VIRGIN SEA OF COCOS ISLAND, FIVE HUNDRED MILES OFF PANAMA

PLATE I

Tales of
FISHING VIRGIN
SEAS

by
ZANE GREY

THE DERRYDALE PRESS
LANHAM AND NEW YORK

THE DERRYDALE PRESS

Published in the United States of America
by The Derrydale Press
4720 Boston Way, Lanham, Maryland 20706

Distributed by NATIONAL BOOK NETWORK, INC.

Library of Congress Cataloging-in-Publication Data

Grey, Zane, 1872-1939.
    Tales of fishing virgin seas / by Zane Grey ; with 100 illustrations from
photographs by the author and other drawings by Lillian Wilhelm Smith.
      p. cm.
    Originally published: New York : Harper & Brothers, 1925.
    ISBN 1-56833-159-2 (pbk. : alk. paper)
    1. Saltwater fishing. 2. Grey, Zane, 1872-1939—Journeys. I. Title.
SH457.G7 2000
799.1'6—dc21   99-087048
                                              CIP

ILLUSTRATIONS

CHAPTER I

A FISHERMAN has many dreams, and from boy-
hood one of mine was to own a beautiful white
ship with sails like wings, and to sail into lonely
tropic seas.

Sometimes dreams, even those of a fisherman, come
true. In August, 1924, I bought a big three-masted
schooner that, of the many vessels along the south shore
of Nova Scotia, appeared to be the finest, and the most
wonderful bargain. She had been built near Lunenburg
five years before, and was one of the stanchest ships sailing from that seafaring port. The four skippers who had
been master of her were loud in praise of her seaworthi-
ness and speed. She had to her credit a record run from
New York to Halifax, and that without a cargo. She
had been twice across the Atlantic. Fortunately for
me she had never been used as a rum-runner, as had
practically all the ships I inspected. I would not have
taken a bootlegger's vessel as a gift.

Her length was one hundred and ninety feet over all,
with beam of thirty-five feet, and she drew eleven feet
six inches of water. I changed the name *Marshal Foch*
to that of *Fisherman*, and left my boatman, Captain Sid
Boerstler, in charge to make the extensive changes we
had planned. The work employed a large force of men
for over three months.

Before I left Nova Scotia I selected a sailing-master

for the ship, and did so perhaps without as much caution as should have been exercised. Captain Sid had the engineers come on from Avalon, and he chose the crew from the Nova Scotia herring fleet, and the first and second mates from the Gloucester swordfish schooner fishermen.

The *Fisherman* left Lunenburg, Nova Scotia, early in December, 1924, and soon ran into the terrific gales then raging the Atlantic. The run to Santiago, Cuba, took twelve days. The next run was to Jamaica. From here the master set a course for Colon, Panama, and on the second morning out, despite the protests of his officers, endeavored to run between some dangerous reefs and went aground. While trying to work the ship off, canoes full of half-savage natives living on the islands in that part of the Caribbean Sea came out to loot the ship. Fortunately she was backed off with apparently little damage before the negroes could board her. At that, Captain Sid said he had his rifle ready. At Colon the ship was put in dry-dock, where it turned out she had stripped her keel. I was notified by cable to discharge the master and put Captain Sid in his place. Both the first and second officers were good navigators, a circumstance Captain Sid had wisely met. They reached Balboa, the Pacific end of the Panama Canal, on January 17th, two days before I sailed from Los Angeles on the S.S. *Manchuria.*

We had a wonderful voyage down the coast for nine days, only one of which was rough. Often we were within sight of land. Off Magdalena Bay, Lower California, we saw twenty-four broadbill swordfish in one day. Farther down, in calm weather, we began to sight small whales, turtles, and sailfish, and large schools of small brown-and-white porpoises, notable for their singular leaping proclivities. Occasionally one would leap out and whirl sidewise with a wrestling motion, something

[2]

new to me. We saw many sailfish off Acapulca, Mexico, in which vicinity the ship officers informed me they sometimes saw thousands of sharks and swordfish. I was pretty well convinced that most ship captains cannot tell the difference between these fish.

Off the coast of Panama many beautiful tropical islands, some with high peaks, charmed our eyes, after so many glaring days on the wide barren sea. We passed the cape lighthouse about dark, and entered Panama Bay. Next morning when we awoke we were docked at Balboa.

I found my ship *Fisherman* something to explore, and more satisfactory than I had dared hope. Here at least was objective proof of my investment, and something worth possessing. The after-cabin had been built to extend over the forward hatch, and it contained eight staterooms and saloon. Galley and crew quarters were new. Below deck there was a combination saloon and dining room, four bathrooms, a dark-room for photography, tackle room, storerooms, a large refrigerator plant, half a dozen staterooms; and back of these the engine room, which had been Captain Sid's particular care and pride. It contained the two Fairbanks-Morse driving engines, an engine to generate electricity for the lights and fans, another for the compressed air that forced water over the ship, an emergency engine to use in case of accident to the electric generator, and automatic pumps and devices. The tanks were all built of steel, and fitted into the sides of the vessel. There were tanks for five thousand gallons of crude oil and one for cylinder oil; tanks for five thousand gallons of water and twenty-five hundred gallons of gasoline. In the forecastle was an engine to hoist sails and anchors; there were lathes, tool bench, forge, and carpenter shop.

[3]

The *Fisherman* carried three launches, one swung over the stern, lashed fast, the other two in cradles on the main deck between the main and mizzen masts. These were launches upon which there had been spent much thought and work. They were intended to be an improvement upon the little boat we had sent to Nova Scotia and which had proved so successful with the giant tuna. These launches were built by MacAlpine of Shelburne, after the famous Cape model so long used to battle the high tides and rough seas of the Bay of Fundy. They were thirty-two and twenty-five feet, respectively, round bottomed, long and slim, and solid as a rock. The keels had been built particularly heavy so that iron bolts holding rings would furnish means by which they could be swung up on deck of the *Fisherman*. Both boats had two New Jersey motors and two propellers, and various other features we had found good in different style models. This time with the California, Florida, and New Jersey features we combined several of Nova Scotia.

For catching fish and battling the monsters of tropic seas we had every kind of tackle that money could buy and ingenuity devise.

The crew and two mates had been Nova Scotia fishermen and sailors all their days. Bob King, from Florida, was again with me, and this man had no peer in the use of cast net and gill net, in finding fish of any species and catching them. Captain Sid had spent six years with me in pursuit of Marlin swordfish, tuna and broadbill. R. C., of course, was in my party, and my son Romer; also George Takahashi, my invaluable genius for all kinds of needs, and Chester Wortley, Mr. Lasky's favorite motion-picture camera operator; and Jess R. Smith, cowboy and horse-wrangler, straight from the Arizona desert, his artist wife, her sister Mrs. Phillips Carlin, and Miss Millicent Smith from New York, Romer's friend,

[4]

YACHT "FISHERMAN" ANCHORED AT COCOS ISLAND

PLATE II

Sea Cave Worn Through Point of Cocos Island

PLATE III

Johnny Shields from Avalon, was along; and lastly Capt. Laurie Mitchell, the English sportsman and an officer in the late war.

As this cruise was the most ambitious and hazardous and the most fascinating adventure I had ever planned, it was natural that I should endeavor to get the best equipment obtainable and as carefully select my companions. At the last moment, almost, the doctor and scientist I had engaged had been compelled to give up the trip, making it necessary for me to act in this capacity.

The long plan had come to fruition; the work had been done, all difficulties met; we were on board with ship and crew ready.

> "The vessel puffs her sails:
> There gloom the broad dark seas."

CHAPTER II

AT eleven-thirty A.M. on the morning of January 30th, we cleared from Balboa, dropped the pilot at the end of the buoys, and were soon out upon the waters of the bay.

The sea was rippling, and the breeze was refreshing after the moist heat of the Canal Zone. At three o'clock the soft green islands sank and vanished in the sea. Next morning we were out of Panama Bay, headed southwest over the lonely lanes of the Pacific. We did not see a steamship or a sailboat. Before the sun set that night I began to appreciate the vast waste of the ocean.

Next day we had a strong breeze that ruffled up a white sea, and we went bowling along at eight knots, without the engines. "Rolled to larboard, rolled to starboard." It took hours for me to grow accustomed to the motion of a sailing ship. How slow and stately she rose and fell, and rolled! The great tall spars with their huge sails seemed to reach to the skies. I walked the deck and sat here and there, always looking. It was a lonely sea. That night a wisp of a moon shone out of the dark blue. Later the stars appeared new or out of place for me.

On the following morning I was awakened by heavy sousing splashes outside my stateroom window. I looked out in time to see a big leathery blackfish leap out high and plunge back. Then yells from R. C. and Romer called me hurriedly on deck. A school of blackfish had accompanied the ship for hours, so the mate said. They played around and ahead of us, sometimes leaping, and riding the swells close to the ship. They were not the balloon-nosed blackfish common to Catalina waters in summer. These were longer, shinier, lighter-colored fish, with a short dorsal, instead of the long hooked one we were familiar with. They were smaller fish, and more agile, sometimes leaping fully thirty feet.

The sea grew calmer as the day advanced, until it was almost smooth. The water began to grow beautifully blue, and its temperature was eighty-five degrees. That amazed me. It was too warm to enjoy a shower-bath.

Fish were scarce. Romer and Johnny rigged up a trolling line, with a hook and white rag, and a tin can at the boat end to draw their attention should they get a strike. It soon came. They hooked a beautiful dolphin that leaped repeatedly before it was drawn in. It was the largest and most colorful I ever saw, weighing about thirty pounds, and a glorious blaze of gold thickly spotted with black. The boys had several strikes after that, and finally lost the trolling line.

We came into a zone where sea birds showed occasionally, all of which were new to me. A dull-gray gull, long and graceful, flew close to the ship, plainly curious. We espied large white-and-black birds, with long bills, that I imagined might be albatross, but could not get near enough to classify them.

The sunset was beyond words to describe. Golden fire, edged about by purple clouds! Then the tropic dusk fell quickly and the silver moon shone straight above the dark sails and the spear-tipped spars. The motion of the ship was stately and beautiful, and the soft ripple of water, the creak of the booms, the flap of canvas, were strange to me. I stayed on deck for hours. It was something staggering to realize where I was, and to look out across the dim, pale, mysterious sea. The worries and troubles incident to this long-planned-for trip began to slough off my mind and to leave me with gradually mounting sensations of awe and wonder and joy. I was going down the grand old Pacific; and there was promise of adventure, beauty, discovery.

On the morning of the fourth day we were five hundred miles out in the Pacific, sailing a dark blue sea, where birds and fish began to grow numerous. Our first destination was Cocos Island, one of the least known spots in all the Seven Seas. If Captain Sid and our navigators had laid a correct course we should be somewhere in the vicinity of this tropic island. The three had worked carefully with instruments and charts, and were confident we had not drifted far from the course.

Naturally crew and passengers kept a sharp lookout for land. Bob climbed aloft several times; and one of the sailors, a brawny fellow, ascended the forward ladder to the crow's-nest, and then, like a monkey, climbed the topsail spar clear to the end. It was wonderful to see him. He remained there for several moments before he descended. I observed that he climbed with his knees as well as with hands.

A half hour later I climbed the rigging almost to the top, and scanned the horizon. It was somewhat a fearful place to stand, so high above decks and swaying with the motion out over the sea, but despite some dizziness and nausea I clung there. The trade-wind clouds along the horizon were deceiving, and many were the formations that fooled me. But at last dead ahead, dim and far distant, I espied a sharp black peak. What a tremendous thrill the sight gave me! I was so surprised by the emotion that at first I could not cry out. I thought of the shipwrecked sailors at last seeing land, and Christopher Columbus at first sight of San Salvador. It was a new and beautiful feeling.

ROMER GREY WITH 50-POUND WAHOO CAUGHT AT COCOS ISLAND

PLATE IV

Romer Grey with 50-pound Wahoo, Caught at Cocos Island

PLATE V

"Land ho! Land ho!" I yelled, and everybody below shouted back at me.

I stayed up there as long as I could stand the dizzy height, and then descended to congratulate my navigators. It was no easy task to hit a small island over five hundred miles out at sea.

"About thirty-five miles," said Captain Sid, beaming with delight. "We'll drop anchor there before sunset."

A school of bonita showed on the surface, leaping and playing; and presently scared up myriads of tiny flying-fish, to which they gave chase.

Romer and Johnny were the happiest of boys, and their expressions of pleasure presupposed an idea that they had not been so sure we would ever find Cocos Island.

"Fine!" ejaculated George Takahashi, his broad brown face wreathed in a grin. "Feel more better now!"

I watched the dim dark peak of land rise out of the sea. Slowly it took on the shape of a mountain, with a sharp point against the sky and precipitous bluffs. How far away! We must have been fifty miles distant when I sighted it. Three o'clock, four o'clock, and still the island seemed unattainable.

Towards five o'clock a long tumbled mass of trade-wind clouds gathered form and color, the blackest and heaviest part of which lodged against the peak. We ran on in, still under both sail and power. When perhaps five miles off the island we sighted an enormous flock of frigate birds sailing round and round over a breaking school of fish. I saw leaping tuna if ever I saw them, and other kinds of fish. All around us fish were breaking water. Then the sun turned gold and red behind the broken clouds. In a few moments I was spellbound with the marvelous spectacle of a sunset turning the sea to a golden quivering jewel. North and east the huge clouds stood up in columns rosy and white. And the island grew.

We dropped the sails and slowed the engines. After sunset dusk fell swiftly, but still there was light on the water. Black and wild the island loomed. A bluff point detached itself from the island and became a smaller island. We made out dark green foliage, pale rocks, and white lines of surf.

It looked risky running in there. But we had a chart that told of deep water and safe anchorage in a cove. Captain Sid ordered the engines stopped. We glided on and on. How rugged the high round ridges above us! The ship rolled on a great ground swell. We passed the outside island and the channel between that and the main island. The moon now shone white on a scene of surpassing loveliness. A strange new sweet fragrance floated from off shore. It was tropic, the scent of sea and jungle. When the sounding lead showed seventeen fathoms Captain Sid ordered the anchor dropped. With rattle and crash it went down. Gradually the ship swung round head to the light wind and ground swell. We were anchored off Cocos Island. It seemed incredible. I was deeply moved. The low boom of surf on rocks filled my ears, and occasionally I caught a low hum of myriads of insects. We caught sight of a dim beach.

No sooner had the vessel answered to her anchor than Johnny and Romer dropped fishing lines and baits over the side. Soon their yells attested to strikes. Crew and all of us ran to see the fun. Romer lost his fish, and Johnny, after quite a battle, hauled up a four-foot shark, wide-sided and bronze-backed. Presently it broke away. Then the boys tried again.

The wildness and loveliness of the place seemed infinitely soul-satisfying to me, and I cared for nothing but to look and listen and feel apart from any companions. There gleamed the vast Pacific, and behind loomed Cocos Island, one of the lost places at the end of the world.

CHAPTER III

ISLE DEL COCOS (Island of Nuts) has long been famed in vague and romantic story as a rendezvous for pirates.

In 1688 an English pirate named Davis gathered together on the island of Hispanola, in the West Indies, a group of hardy sea-rovers, from whom, no doubt, Stevenson created his great romance, *Treasure Island*. Davis planned a daring voyage round the Horn, and eventually discovered Cocos Island, more than five hundred miles off the Costa Rican coast. This Pacific island must not be mistaken for the Cocos Islands in the Indian Ocean.

Davis and his pirates captured a Danish vessel, which they took for their raids. They sacked ships and burned towns, between which depredations they sought refuge at Cocos Island. From this objective point, almost unknown then, Davis ravaged the coast of Peru. Most of the immense treasure he amassed was buried on Cocos Island. History does not record that he carried much of it to England.

In 1820, during a revolution in Peru, many rich Spaniards gave in charge to a Captain Thompson over twelve million dollars in jewels and gold, which he buried on Cocos Island. Later he became a pirate, no doubt for the express purpose of stealing the treasure that had been intrusted to him. But it was never known that he was able to get back to Cocos Island. When the

Wreck Bay at Cocos Island. Scene of Numerous Treasure-hunting Expeditions

PLATE VI

Forty-eight-pound Crevalle, Purple and Silver Color, Very Vivid and Beautiful

PLATE VII

pirate Bonito was captured Thompson escaped, eventually to get on board a ship bound for Newfoundland. There he interested treasure-seekers to outfit a ship to go to Cocos Island. But he died before the ship sailed. He left, however, a carefully drawn map of the hiding place of the buried treasure; and through that several expeditions have visited Cocos Island. Only one adventurer was ever known to find treasure on the tropic island, and this was a man named Keating, who, after fights with the crew he sought to cheat, finally got away alone in a boat with a hundred thousand dollars' worth of jewels and gold.

As late as 1924 a treasure-hunting ship dropped anchor off Cocos Island, and the adventurers made an exhaustive search of certain sections, all to no avail.

Daylight found me on deck of the *Fisherman* with the above romance of the pirates and treasure-seekers in mind, and as I saw the wild, precipitous cliffs, green with flowing moss, and the rugged caverns, I thought it no wonder the treasure had never been found.

The morning was softly gray with pearly clouds hiding the sun. Myriads of wild fowl wheeled above the ship and the huge gray rock that loomed out from the mainland. Such a bright-green foliage I had never seen before. Palm trees stood out against the sky line; the steep slopes showed pale bare-stemmed trees with lacy spreading tops; tree ferns stood above the massed vines that swept down the rock-faced wall to the sea. There was a small white curved beach where a stream of water poured out of the jungle. The air was full of the strange sweet scent that I had noted so keenly the night before. I saw myriads of flowers peeping out of the vines. And the large white dots, that at first I took for blossoms, turned out to be young birds on their nests.

[13]

The sun came out at intervals, and it was hot. We worked on tackle while the crew endeavored to get the launches overboard. It was a hard, risky job and was not completed until two o'clock, and then not without damage to our precious fishing boats.

Meanwhile Romer and Johnny, with Captain Mitchell, had gone out in the small boat, and had at once become engaged with some kind of hard-fighting fish. Presently Sid had the launch ready for Chester, and Bob performed a like task for R. C. and me with the thirty-two-foot launch.

The sun was hidden by clouds; a brisk breeze was whipping up whitecaps outside the bay. We ran out a few hundred yards, by which time R. C. and I had light-tackle lines overboard.

I saw a swirl, a flash of yellow, a splash behind R. C.'s feathered jig. He hooked something that was off like a shot. Bob threw out the clutch. But R. C. could not stop the fish. It ran off four hundred and fifty yards of line in a few seconds, and snap! Every foot of the line gone! Just a moment later I had a smashing strike, and hooked a heavy fish that broke my line. Then we resorted to heavier tackle. R. C. had another strike and missed. I saw long, slender, silvery needlefish leaping like greyhounds across the dark-blue water. It was a little too rough for comfort.

A flock of frigate birds and boobies swept down upon us, and utterly devoid of fear they began to swoop down to try to pick up our baits. It was a thrilling, beautiful sight—the gray, smooth, sharp-billed, sharp-tailed boobies, and the big, black, white-breasted, bow-winged frigate birds, sailing, wheeling, darting down over our baits. R. C. was using a feathered jig, which they left alone. My bait was a strip of cut fish, and these sea birds were hungry. Time and again one would pick it up and sail

[14]

away, with others fighting him, while I reeled and pulled to get my bait free. Chester followed closely in the other boat, having a fine chance for an unusual picture. Finally one hungry frigate bird caught my hook in the tip of his beak. Then I had a fight with a bird-fish. He soared while I reeled slowly. All the other birds flocked about this one I had hooked, screaming and squawking. I reeled him down to Bob's outstretched hands, and soon he was liberated. But he wheeled at once to join the others in frantic endeavor to get our baits. We had to quit fishing until they got tired following our boat and flew away.

Then we ran up into the channel between the great black rock and the mainland of the island. This channel was deep, swift, darkly violet in hue, and it boomed in swelling surges against the perpendicular cavernous bluffs. The rock was limestone and a magnificent monument, infinitely beautiful with its rough gray face patched by graceful groups of trees upon which birds were nesting. A thousand birds were wheeling and circling the lofty summit.

I hooked several fish that got free in short order. Then R. C. connected with one that he soon landed. It was a yellowtail of perhaps twenty pounds, a most beautiful long slim fish, with one yellow and one blue stripe running down its sides. In shape it resembled the racy clean-cut kingfish of Florida waters.

I had missed Romer and Johnny for some time, and as the thundering surges piling up on the stone walls frightened me considerably I gave up fishing to look for their boat. Finally we located them, away across the arm of another bay and between another island and the mainland. We ran over there. This island proved to be a bird rock. It stood up two hundred feet and more above the sea, and its steep gray broken slopes were spotted with bird nests. On top stood a line of boobies, and above in the air hundreds were sailing around.

The mainland here presented a magnificent precipice a thousand feet high, almost straight up, exquisitely softly green with lacy vines, creepers, moss, and out of these shining the pale-barked trees. A silvery waterfall, like smoke, slipped out of a niche high up, and tumbling down, dividing the green clear to the sea. I saw great caverns so dark and huge, so beset by thundering surges of green-white billows, that they fascinated me beyond full appreciation. It would take time to see and understand this wild Cocos Island.

We reached Romer and Johnny and got them turned back toward the ship. When we arrived there, and after considerable effort were safely on board again, we listened to a remarkable fish story from these youngsters, and saw enough in the fish they brought back to compel us to believe most of it. They had broken a good many lines on big fish. They had nine crevalle, one amber-jack, one grouper, one muttonfish, all of considerable size, some of them over fifteen pounds. The crevalle were pale blue and purple, and the other fish colored proportionately, so that only by their shape could I recognize their species, and then I was not absolutely sure. The shark stories these boys told were scarcely credible, until later, when some one threw fish overboard, to bring up great yellow monsters with silver-edged fins, beautiful, uncanny creatures of the deep that fought one another right under our eyes, I was convinced. It gave me a chill to watch them. While several were fighting over a piece of fish a huge yellowtail, the largest I ever saw, darted in to seize a share and escape with it.

The sunset over the point of mountain and the channel between it and the great Bird Rock was one of tropic splendor—massed cumulus clouds with silver edges and

MAN-OF-WAR HAWKS AT COCOS ISLAND (Plates viii to xi)

(*These birds stole our fish-baits, making it impossible to fish.*)

PLATE VIII

PLATE IX

Plate x

PLATE XI

golden rays, and sky of shell pink. The warmth and intensity of colors marked the difference between this sunset and those I was familiar with north.

Dark clouds rolled over the island, and by night rain was falling, lightly and mistily at first, but gradually increasing until it roared on the canvas and the decks. I went out to look. All was gray pall. The island showed dim, mysterious, vague, and the sea moaned hauntingly.

What a far-away place, lost in the vast Pacific! But it had its strong and incessant life, its resistless forces of nature, its processes of evolution and decay.

During the night the ship rolled and rocked, from one side far over to the other; and booms rattled, chains creaked, and loose objects on deck clattered about. Yet I soon fell asleep and did not awaken until gray dawn. It came cool, wet, dark, with the surges pounding on the rocks, in an echoing circle all around the bay.

CHAPTER IV

MORNING came, cool, dark, gray, with broken clouds round the horizon, and a veil of mist over the island. The foliage appeared drenched. In the east a low clear belt of sky, dark-rose in hue, showed where the sun had risen.

After breakfast a wind arose, rather stiff, right out of the east, and it kicked up whitecaps, and a swell that caused the *Fisherman* to career over on her side and swing back again. Everything loose in the big ship went helter-skelter.

It was not long, however, until the wind abated and the sun gave promise of shining. Romer and Johnny took to their little boat and had not fished a hundred yards before they had something on. I watched this battle, and it was highly diverting. When Johnny drew the quarry near the boat Romer laid down his gaff and whipped a rifle to begin shooting into the water, manifestly at a shark. Presently they captured a fish, a fine large yellowtail. I began to form an impression as to the business-like ability of the boys.

When the sea flattened somewhat, R. C. and I took the large launch, and with Sid and Chester following we ran out to sea. About a mile out R. C. had a vicious strike and hooked a fast fish. It ran away, then back; and presently we saw a bulge on the water behind it. R. C. literally pulled his fish away from a shark. It was an albacore, of about eighteen pounds, and had considerable of yellow and gold color. Then I had a strike and missed.

We ran out several miles. The sun emerged from the cloud-bank, and then we knew it was to be hot. We were bathed in sweat without moving a muscle. Then I had the luck to hook a big heavy fish. He went down, taking several hundred yards of line before I could stop him. Both of us had seen the strike, but not the fish. It did not act like a shark. I had hooked it on a light rod, with number twelve line, and I began to work hard. That rod certainly took punishment. But I could not get the fish up. In perhaps a quarter of an hour I decided I had hooked a good-sized tuna. Yet I could only surmise. Later in the day, however, when R. C. saw two large long-fin tuna, probably the Allison tuna, I was sure of that fish I fought. We will never know, because he broke my line. Half an hour pumping on that fish, in the broiling sun, had exhausted me and made me as wet as if I had fallen into the ocean.

We had no more luck, and soon ran back to the ship. The shade was certainly welcome. Any unprotected place on the ship, if touched by the hand, burned like fire.

After lunch we manned the three boats and set out for what was called Wreck Bay, several miles round to the westward. The course lay under the precipitous cliffs, vine-festooned and moss-mantled, and between white surge-begirt islands and headlands, where the countless wild fowl screamed and wheeled. How the surf thundered on the black walls! The violet sea rose and fell in vast heaves, chafing at its iron-bound confines, and booming in deep hollow sullen roar.

We turned a cape, lofty and jungle-covered, to be confronted by a grand spectacle of the bold heights of Cocos Island. Across a wide bay the green walls rose to the dignity of mountain range, and from a lofty canyon pitched a lacy white waterfall, "like downward smoke," that seemed to pause and fall and pause again. It was

[19]

three hundred feet high, and all that was needed to make that scene perfect.

The bay cut deep into the island, and as we ran on, turning another corner, we came to where a white curved beach smiled in the sunlight, and cocoanut palms bordered the edge of the jungle. Here at a low point a stream ran out into the sea, and it appeared to come from a valley of luxuriant jungle growths. We went ashore in the canoes, and for the first time in my life I felt like Crusoe on his lonely isle. There was the remains of an old shack where a gold-seeker had once lived, and to disappear, as the story goes, never to be heard of again. We spent three hours along this crescent beach, and were loath to leave. I could not quite grasp the spell of the place. But perhaps it would come to me. The stream was swift, clear, cold, and a joy to the parched visitor, whether mariner or fisherman. The cocoanut palms were very slender and tall, with pearl-gray stems and small tufted heads. But they were undoubtedly fruit-bearing cocoanut palms, and lent the spot not a little of its sum of paradise. Great red agaves shone on some of the broad shiny-leaved trees; tree-ferns spread wide fans down from the vine-covered bluff above the stream; many lofty trees wore a wreath of vines clear to the top, where the branches spread. Far up a slope, dense, tropic, exotic, showed trees with bright-red parasites. Flowers bloomed everywhere, and the only blossom I could recognize was a tiny pink morning-glory. Some blossoms were huge and orange in hue. Back along the stream there was a tangled, impenetrable jungle, green and white and gold. Down upon this verdant valley, shut in by the green walls, poured the hot sun. The sand was too hot for the bare foot. The wild fowl sailed low and high, everywhere, some almost invisible up in the blue sky. Up the strand curled three shallow lines of surf, white-

[20]

crested, green-hollowed, with low crashing roar, to break and spread up the beach. The purple bay reached out to the heaving sea. Sweet, strange was the perfume, resembling that of a hothouse. The breeze in the palms bore inexplicable tidings to me. This was a tropic world and I was a stranger.

Johnny and Romer returned from a hunt up the stream, wet and dirty, beaming of face, babbling about wild pigs, strange tracks, green spiders, golden birds. But they did not bring any game.

Wreck Bay was a hard place to leave. I want to go again, to have longer to stay, to watch the waterfall from the green mountain, and the slow movement of the purple bay, and the ever-present haunting cries and flight of the wild fowl.

On the way back we trolled for yellowtail. I saw Romer and Johnny hook several, to meet with disaster. Then, off the sharp head of an island, where the surge mounted high and white, I had my rod almost jerked out of my hands. The fish made a long run. We followed. I got my line back, and was drawing him close when a terrific irresistible force attached itself to the end of my line and shot away. Shark! I could do nothing. The line whizzed off the reel. These Cocos Island sharks were as fast as swordfish. This one soon broke my line. Then I gave up for the day.

On the way back we gathered the wild fowl round us again, so close that we could almost touch them, and their sailing flights and strange cries and absolute indifference to the presence of man, repaid fully for the futility of the fishing.

Another day was clear and hot, with very little breeze. The sea was calm, yet great ground swells rolled in from the sea, making the ship keel over so far that it was hard to keep upright.

We ran round beyond Wreck Bay to fish near the waterfall, and take pictures against that beautiful background. White cloud-ships sailed the azure sky, and cast moving shadows along the vivid green slopes.

R. C. and I began to troll with cut bait a little way off shore under the looming mountain. We forgot the beauty of the scene. The green-purple sea was alive with fish, and the air with birds, both of which made frantic efforts to steal the baits from our hooks. In truth the swift frigate birds were more adept at snatching our baits than the yellowtail, crevalle, turbot, and other fish, including sharks, were in getting them. But the birds were absolutely fearless, and the fish showed some little caution. I actually saw a frigate bird snatch my bait right out of the jaws of a fish. For a second both had hold of it.

Whenever I did hook a fish the birds soon soared upward again, to wheel along the green cliffs. Here the water was not more than thirty feet deep and the bottom could be seen distinctly. It was a veritable marine garden, with dark gray shadows of sharks moving over the opal-hued rocks. If I failed to haul in a fish very quickly he became fodder for the sharks.

After a time we grew sick of this carnage and ran west a mile, and out into the sea where a ragged rock stood up lonesomely, begirt by white wreaths of surf. Here the water was very deep, and a dark purple in hue. When we ran in close to the rock, within fifty feet, which was pretty risky, we could see the gold and amber rocks, and myriads of fish.

R. C. put a bait over. A swarm of blue-sided, purple-striped crevalle appeared, and among them gleamed the long beautifully slim and striped shapes of yellowtail. They appeared to run from fifteen pounds up, to thirty

for the crevalle and twice that, perhaps, for the yellowtail. What a wonderful aquarium! R. C. hooked a fish
at once, and the fight was on. We had decided light
tackle was foolish and cruel, as we could not hope to
land even one fish. With heavy tackle we hoped to work
very hard and beat the sharks. R. C. brought a crevalle
to the boat in record time. Behind it flashed a bronze-
backed shark with black silver-tipped fins and tail, and
he rushed so fast that he splashed water all over Bob, who
had bent to lift R. C.'s crevalle out. The shark thumped
the boat. He was about ten feet long and might have
weighed three hundred pounds. He acted very much as
if he had been cheated out of his dinner.

"Well, the peevish son-of-a-gun!" ejaculated R. C.
"What do you know about that?"

"I know I'm going to put the hickory on some of these
sea-hogs," I replied, grimly.

That was when we took to the tuna tackle. I trolled
a bait about twenty feet. A school of beautiful turbot,
velvet dark in color with blue stripes, churned the water
back of my bait. Blue gleams, green flashes! Then a
broad bar of bronze! Smash! A shark hit that bait as
clean and hard as any tarpon or marlin I ever saw. He
made a long run and cut my line.

"Doggone!" I complained. "That was one of my air-
plane leaders. This is getting expensive."

"We're goin' to the funeral of some of these heah
sharks," declared Bob King, with fire in his eye.

The next hour was so full of fish that I could never tell
actually what did happen. We had hold of some big
crevalle, and at least one enormous yellowtail, perhaps
seventy-five pounds. But the instant we hooked one,
great swift gray and green shadows appeared out of
obscurity. We never got a fish near the boat. Such
angling got on my nerves. It was a marvelous sight to

[23]

peer down into that exquisitely clear water and see fish as thickly laid as fence pickets, and the deeper down the larger they showed. All kinds of fish lived together down there. We saw yellowtail and amberjack swim among the sharks as if they were all friendly. But the instant we hooked a poor luckless fish he was set upon by these voracious monsters and devoured. They fought like wolves. Whenever the blood of a fish discolored the water these sharks seemed to grow frantic. They appeared on all sides, as if by magic.

By and by we had sharks of all sizes swimming round under our boat. One appeared to be about twelve feet long or more, and big as a barrel. There were only two kinds, the yellow sharp-nosed species, and the bronze shark with black fins, silver-edged. He was almost as grand as a swordfish.

While trying to get the big fellow to take a bait I hooked and whipped three of this bunch, the largest one being about two hundred and fifty pounds. It did not take me long to whip them, once I got a hook into their hideous jaws. The largest, however, did not get to my bait.

An interesting and grewsome sight was presented when Bob, after dismembering one I had caught, tumbled the bloody carcass back into the water. It sank. A cloud of blood spread like smoke. Then I watched a performance that beggared description. Sharks came thick upon the scene from everywhere. Some far down seemed as long as our boat. They massed around the carcass of their slain comrade, and a terrible battle ensued. Such swift action, such ferocity, such unparalleled instinct to kill and eat! But this was a tropic sea, with water at eighty-five degrees, where life is so intensely developed. Slowly that yellow flashing, churning mass of sharks faded into the green depths.

[24]

The Beautiful Shore Line of Tropic Cocos Island

PLATE XII

Where the Lacy White Waterfalls, Like Downward Smoke, Poured
from the Green Blossoming Cliffs

PLATE XIII

R. C. looked at me and I looked at him. We both had the same realization. Fishing for game fish, to which he and I had so long devoted ourselves, was almost an impossibility in these tropic seas. The fish were there, more abundant by far than our wildest dreams had pictured, but they could not be fought in a sportsmanlike way and landed.

Strife in this hot ocean was intensely magnified, in proportion to the enormous number of fish. Nature had developed them to be swifter, fiercer, stronger than fish in northern seas. It struck me strangely that there had not been any sign of fish feeding on the surface, such as was so familiar to our eyes in Florida, California, and Nova Scotia waters. Yet here there were a million times more fish, little and big! The upper stratum of water was hot, and all species of fish remained below it, until something unusual brought them up. Tremendous contending strife went on below the beautiful blue surface of the Pacific. It seemed appallingly deceitful. The beauty was there to see, but not the joy of life. I had not observed any fish leaping in play.

As we decided not to make an extended stay at Cocos Island the boys did not want to waste any opportunities. They were fishing again soon after sunrise. I stood on the deck of the ship and watched them with Captain Mitchell trolling around the bay. When presently Romer hooked a fish that made a tremendous splash I concluded it was a shark. But as I kept on watching my conviction weakened. These sharks about Cocos Island, however, were so fast and savage, so much like the gamest of fish, that it was impossible to judge what actions they could or would perform. At any rate, Romer had a hard battle with the fish he had hooked, chasing it all over the bay. I did not see the finish. But soon Romer came speeding back in the launch, wild with excitement. "Hey, dad!" he yelled, his brown face shining in the sun. "Just caught the most wonderful fish. Terrible scrapper! Look!"

The boatman with evident labor held up a long slim dark fish with pointed nose and great broad tail, and a low straight dorsal fin that reached far down its back.

"Wahoo!" I yelled, amazed. "Sure as you're born. It's a wahoo, Romer, and a whopper!"

They brought the fish on board, where we had a good close look at it. I did not know that wahoo, or "peto," as this species is called in the West Indies, was an inhabitant of the Pacific. Wahoo are fairly often caught in the Bahamas, and rarely in Florida. Years ago I caught the first one ever taken at Long Key. Romer's fish weighed about forty pounds, and he was indeed to be congratulated.

The taking of this wahoo surprised me, and caused me to depart somewhat from my hasty judgment as to its being almost impossible to catch a game fish at Cocos Island. Indeed, failure to see fish feeding on the surface had discouraged me, and this with the actual fact that the sea was alive with sharks had almost influenced me to heave anchor and sail for the Galapagos.

Most of the clouds rolled away, and this, with the absence of wind, made the day exceedingly hot. Nevertheless we worked all morning, mostly at photographing birds.

Early in the afternoon R. C. rigged up his big swordfish tackle, and I took Romer with me, and Sid, Johnny, Captain Mitchell, and Jess went in the small boat. We ran out of the bay a mile or more, and turned east. I let Romer use the heavy tackle. First we tried a No. 6 Wilson spoon, and they put on one of the big tarporenos.

They make clumsy bludgeon kind of baits, but are attractive to fish.

We trolled down a mile or more, and upon turning to go back saw R. C. fighting a fish some distance out. As we ran toward his boat I was attracted by a flock of boobies, swirling, wheeling, darting all around him. Then I saw breaks on the water. A dark bullet-shaped fish leaped high, with quivering tail, coming out of the water like an arrow.

"Tuna! Tuna!" I yelled. "Run over there, Sid."

Romer was wild with excitement and kept babbling at a great rate. We reached R. C. in time to see him pulling strenuously on a fish. The big tackle was the thing for this shark-infested ocean. He pulled the leader to Bob, and Bob hauled on it, and lifted out a fine yellow-fin tuna that thumped over into the boat and nearly threw the fishermen out.

"School of yellow-fin," shouted R. C., wiping his dripping red face. "All around us. Saw two that would go nearly three hundred pounds. Look down!"

Sure enough I saw some swift darkly yellow fish that faded away in the purple depths.

All this time Romer had left his tarporeno in the water, and it sank, of course, as our launch slowed down. Suddenly he had a terrific strike.

"Oh! Oh!" screamed Romer, hanging on to the wagging rod.

It was indeed a tuna strike, and that it was from a very large fish I had no doubt. The first run took two hundred yards of line off the reel. Romer could not stop him. On the second run the fish tore loose from the hook. As I looked back I was in time to see R. C. get fast to another.

"Somethin' doin'," called Sid, with a pleased laugh.

"I see some big tuna on the surface. Lots of little ones, too."

We ran back to R. C., and reached him in time to see him pull loose from a heavy fish.

Then things began to happen rather too swiftly for comfort or record. Romer had the luck to have a big yellow-fin sail right up behind the launch, and with thumping splash take the tarporeno off the surface. Romer gave a mighty tug. He hooked the fish, and it broke off. This was a disappointment, but I was afraid the tuna were too heavy and fast for Romer to handle.

He had wonderful luck in getting strikes. In the next few minutes he hooked three more tuna, all big ones, and each broke off, taking tarporeno and leader. We rigged up our last one and put that out. Romer had no time to rest. I saw a flash of yellow, and a swirl; then smash! he was fast to another. This one went straight down, after the manner of most tuna, and with six or seven hundred feet of line out he was hard to move. Romer pulled and puffed and panted, and performed valiantly. But to capture a tuna that day was not for him. This one also got away, by freeing himself from the hook.

We were out of tackle, so had nothing to do but go see how it fared with our comrades. We found Captain Mitchell fighting a tuna. Johnny exhibited some broken tackle and a woeful face.

Farther on, R. C. was laying back with his heavy rod. He surely was in fighting mood. Running down his way, we saw him pull up a twelve-foot shark, that Bob held by the leader while the sailor aboard stabbed it with a long spear. Water scattered everywhere. They made short work of that shark.

"Tuna all around!" called R. C. "I had a big one about licked when the hook pulled out. Tuna everywhere, and a million sharks."

A cloud of darting, diving birds attracted my attention. We ran over to find boobies feeding in a school of small fish that the tuna had driven to the surface. This was a doubly fine spectacle for me. It was the first opportunity I had ever had to watch boobies catch fish. They sailed, darted, wheeled, then closed their wings and pitched straight down, like a plummet, to hit the water hard and go clear out of sight. Sometimes they did not come up quickly. Fish hawks, kingfishers, eagles, frigate birds, terns, gulls I had watched, but none of these could compare with the boobie.

We ran with this flock of birds and school of fish for half an hour, during which time I tried to take photographs, especially of that marvelous dive from high above. Then the school of fish went down and the birds dispersed.

Returning to R. C., we found him again engaged in strenuous battle. There was excitement on board. Bob and the sailor waved at us, and shouted and pointed. I could not see anything but R. C.'s long sweep of rod and powerful pull.

We ran in close. Then I saw dark yellow flashes in the water. Bob was reaching for the leader. He got it and hauled with might and main. A tremendous splashing followed, then rapid sodden flapping on the surface. Dark fins and tails showed out of the maelstrom.

The head of a tuna showed. Bob was pulling like a giant. Higher he lifted. The smashing of water grew fiercer. Then I saw the huge broad nose of a shark that had the tuna in its mouth. Bob was hauling to hold the tuna; the shark was doing likewise; and the other sharks were fighting to get what they could.

The big shark had swallowed the tuna clear to its gills. Suddenly Bob lurched back, swinging the severed head. Then followed a frightful commotion in the water. We moved over still closer, and I was amazed to see a dozen or more large sharks just under the surface, a beautiful yet hideous sight. What color, what command of the water! Bob dangled the head of the tuna on the surface, and the sharks came for it. They were as wild as tigers and yet as approachable as sheep. The sailor jabbed the spear into their heads as they reached for the remains of the tuna. There was one monster of six or eight hundred pounds. He glided to and fro under the others, and I suspected he was the one which had bitten the tuna. We watched them for some time. I saw remoras sticking on some, and large pilot fish on others. The whole spectacle was awesome, grim, and fascinating. I always hated sharks, but I had to admit their necessity in an ocean as procreant as the Pacific. On the way back to the ship I was so thoughtful I scarcely grasped Romer's ravings about what he had done and seen.

After supper we held a council of war, and though we differed in many points, we all agreed on the tremendous quantity of fish and the almost insurmountable obstacle in the way of sharks.

"I wish some of the light-tackle advocates could be here," said R. C. "They would learn a great deal. We might just as well put the light stuff away if we want to save any of it for a more favorable place."

"Well, I advise long leaders and heavy lines. We'll try that for a day or two," I added.

The tuna we caught appeared to be yellow-fins, though differing somewhat from the yellow-fin we have around Clemente Island in September. These were exceedingly handsome fish, very rich in coloring, intensely blue on the back, pearly silver underneath, with iridescent barred sides, large black eyes, and blazing gold toward the tail, especially the small fins and the triangular little rudders. The pectoral fins appeared to be somewhat longer than

First Sight of Galapagos Islands

PLATE XIV

YACHT "FISHERMAN" ANCHORED OFF EDEN ISLAND, GALAPAGOS

PLATE XV

those of the yellow-fin we have off California. I was satisfied this fish never strikes far north.

They were also different from the long-finned tuna R. C. saw from the deck of the ship. These had very long bow-shaped pectorals, and must have been the Hawaiian long-fin, or the Allison tuna. They would have weighed between two and three hundred pounds.

Another feature of our fishing there, that I dwelt considerably on, was the danger from sharks, even while we were in the launches. I gave data of several cases where sharks had caved in the sides of boats, by accident, most likely, and sunk them. Our launches had been made with air-tight compartments and were supposed to be unsinkable. Still we did not want to run any chances. I advised that the sharks should not be gaffed, but shot or speared. It was a risky business and worried me. Still, I had not seen any really enormous sharks. The number, however, that could appear as if by magic, was enough to daunt any angler.

The hazard of this fishing game in the tropics did not on the moment seem as fascinating as I had imagined it might be. Perhaps that was because I felt responsible for everybody, especially my boy Romer, his pal, and R. C.

This thought led my mind to another danger, and that was to risk a ship more than five hundred miles out of the track of steamers and sailing craft. I felt terribly alone. We did not fear storms, for they were rare in this latitude. The thought of fire on board was appalling. I had never been placed in quite such an insecure situation. It would have appealed more to me if I had been without responsibility for others. The lure of virgin seas was irresistible, but it had drawbacks, such as I now faced. Thought and intelligence have considerable power over the primitive in man. That is the hope of progress in the world.

I lay in the hammock on deck and watched the moon soar over the wild black mountain. It shone down through the swinging spars and ropes, a white tropic moon, in a pale green circle that merged into the intense violet of the sky. I never tired of the incessant roar of the surf. The ever-haunting presence of the sea! I realized that I was not feeling the wonder and strangeness of this place as I had felt for places less remote, and far less enchanting. I had a fear complex, and sought to throw it off.

The ship rolled gracefully at her anchorage; the wild fowl flew by, crossing the white moon and dark sky; the surf moaned and thundered; the hum of insects came faintly, with melancholy sweetness. From the sea blew a fresh cool scent that mingled with the fragrance of the jungle island.

CHAPTER V

THE preposterous luck of a beginner is well known to all fishermen. It is an inexplicable thing. Jess Smith had handled thousands of bucking horses and lassoed innumerable wild steers; but when he came to use rod and reel he did not know one end from another. I saw him point the rod as if it were a gun and wind the reel backward. Nevertheless, and marvelous to relate, Jess captured a hundred pound yellow-fin tuna.

It happened this way. I sent Chester with some of the boys to take pictures of birds. I lent Jess one of my best rods, about halfway between heavy and light, and cautioned him to use it only near shore, in shallow water, where large fish were not likely to be struck.

About noon I saw the boats coming back through the channel between Bird Rock and the main island. The small launch halted right in midchannel. Sea fowl were wheeling about over the boat. I concluded some one had hooked a fish, but had no idea that it might be Jess. When Sid arrived in the first launch, however, he brought news that Jess had established connection with a large fish, and was a circus to behold.

"But my fine Leonard rod!" I ejaculated, in dismay.

"Don't you know any better than to lend your good tackle?" retorted Sid, disapprovingly. "Look at Romer and Johnny. They've already used up enough tackle to start a fishing village."

I got my glasses and brought them to bear upon that little boat. It bobbed around so in the swift rough tide-rip that I had difficulty locating it. Sure enough, Jess was on a fish, and, alas! the rod appeared to be wagging like a buggy whip. It dawned upon me presently that the boat was moving and that the object seemed to be to drag the fish out of the tide-rip. I was certain the tackle would not last long, even if the fish did stay on, which possibility appeared infinitesimal. But when from time to time I saw that the boat was working into the bay Jess still had the fish. To my amaze the fish stayed on. From this fact I could only conclude that it must be a shark. Forthwith I went below, and stayed in my stateroom until roused out by yells. Running up on deck, I saw that the little boat with boatman, Captain Mitchell, Takahashi, and Jess had arrived in triumph. Jess was standing up, wet and disheveled, with his mop of hair all straggly, and his shirt out of his trousers and mostly up round his neck. Now Jess was powerful and he had been so long fighting this fish that he had gotten somewhat the knack of pumping and winding. No doubt about his physical and mental condition! In both he was practically a wreck. What a rapt wet face he lifted to his admirers on the ship! Then I realized that he had dragged the fish for nearly an hour, and had performed miracles of endurance, all because he wanted his wife to see him. Proud! He was astounding. I was probably somewhat nettled at the loss of my rod, for it was now a sad sight, but I began to grow out of my selfish attitude. Mrs. Smith was quite interesting. She stood up on the bow and was screaming in delight, while trying to sketch her husband with one hand and photograph him with the other.

"Reckon I've hawg-tied a Texas long-horn!" yelled Jess.

Romer, Johnny, R. C., and the rest of us began to encourage Jess.

"Ride him, cowboy!" yelled Romer.

"Give him the spurs, Jess," added Johnny.

"Hey, Jess," put in R. C., "hang on to the pommel!"

These sallies rejuvenated Jess, and he began to work with a frantic appreciation of his importance and opportunity. His wife had as much of the center of the stage as he.

"Oh, Jess!" she cried, running around with her hands full. "Be careful! You'll fall in. You'll hurt yourself if that fishing pole breaks! Oh, don't lose your fish. You've got to get him!"

Her exclamations were drowned by my stentorian roar.

"Jess, that's not a pole to punch cows with. That's a fishing-rod. . . . Don't pull so hard! Not so far back! . . . Oh, for Heaven's sake, break it quick!"

But Jess did not break my rod quite in two pieces. He merely bent it into a permanent figure S while he hauled up the fish for our edification. How it blazed gold and opal!

"Darned if it isn't a tuna!" ejaculated R. C.

I recognized this, too, but I was so far gone now that I could only watch. It was a good big fish, and though exhausted it still had power to weave in and out. George Takahashi had the gaff, and as he stabbed at the tuna I wanted to yell, but could not. Takahashi made valiant efforts to get the gaff in the tuna.

"Hit him again, George," called R. C., in delight. "Soak him! You're off on your slice stroke."

It certainly was written that the poor tuna was doomed. Eventually amid great splashes and a congested knot of men it was hauled into the launch, and from there brought up to the deck of the ship.

"Worse than—breakin' wild broncos," said Jess. He

was a sight to behold—dirty, ragged, wet, panting, and red in the face. His pleasure was so tremendous that I forgot the ruined rod.

The tuna weighed a little over a hundred pounds, and as it lay on deck I doubted if I had ever seen a more beautiful fish. Gold, silver, purple predominated over many other hues. As in the others we had caught, I marked particularly the large beautiful black eyes. They reminded me somewhat of the eyes of a Florida ladyfish. Another striking feature was the mottled bronze of the body along the sides toward the tail. It seemed almost that the fish was checkered with iridescent spots and bars, quivering, changing, coalescing, fading. The vivid and intense hues were startling to the eye. Bright as had seemed a Nova Scotia tuna, it was indeed dull and drab compared with this glorious creature.

R. C. took Romer out that afternoon, and I went alone in the small launch with Sid. The ocean was dark blue, heaving, rippling under the white blaze of the sun. I used my heaviest tackle, the one on which I caught the seven-hundred-and-fifty-eight-pound Nova Scotia tuna, and a twenty-five-foot leader, the kind used by the mako-shark anglers of New Zealand. My idea was, if I hooked a fish, to haul it in quickly to save it, and also, when I hooked sharks, to subdue them promptly before they could roll up in the leader and saw off the line.

The azure water, into which I could see down deeply, appeared to be untenanted. No fish, no sharks, no birds! Almost I was relieved. But when I let my cut bait back a hundred feet it was seized with a smash. A heavy fish swirled away and surged close under the surface. Shark! I shut down on him and pulled him up to the boat in two minutes, where the boatmen attended to the disagreeable and dangerous task of dispatching it to save hook and leader.

Another bait let out, this time not far, met the same fate; and I grimly hauled in my second shark. That was the beginning of a shark massacre. But as I had determined to fish irrespective of these myriads of sea tigers, there was nothing to do but keep at it.

We drew over close to R. C.'s boat and came abreast of Romer's bait trailing white and alluring through the blue water. I was about to yell a cheery greeting when I saw something flashing back of his bait. It struck me mute. A blaze of golden fire, streaked and crossed with silver rays, moved with wonderful rapidity up to the surface. It was a great yellow-fin tuna. Three hundred—perhaps four hundred pounds! I saw black eyes as large as saucers, and huge jaws that opened to snatch Romer's bait.

The water cracked and opened with a roar. The blaze of gold vanished in white.

"I got one, dad!" screamed Romer, with wild gladness, as he held hard to the nodding rod.

"No, son," I yelled back. "He's got you."

I did not think it could do any good to advise, or to tell Romer what he had hold of. In a few seconds the line was all off the reel, and then the hook pulled out.

That incident stimulated me to renewed patience and persistence. I put another bait over. Bang! This strike came from a tuna, if my judgment was sound. The big tackle stopped him short of four hundred yards. I had a large hook and a long strong leader. For a moment I forgot the almost insurmountable task of capturing a heavy hard-fighting fish in these waters, and I began to work on this one with renewed spirit. He stayed down, no doubt far below the zone of sharks. And while he stayed down there all seemed well. When, however,

I began to get the better of the fish and draw him up, the story was different. I knew when he made a wild rush to escape sharks, and equally well I knew when they caught him. Tugs and jerks and pulls, vibrations and shakings, were the means by which I felt that tuna literally devoured off my hook.

Some time later I was out of bait, tarporenos, spoons, feathered jigs, but I had no fish. The great tackle, however, had accounted for more sharks than I cared to count. I had hooked tuna, albacore, dolphin, yellowtail, and other fish I could not name. There had been several harrowing moments when it seemed I might outwit the sharks and catch a fish. But always when I labored strenuously and gazed with distended eyes down into the clear water, to see my fish with other fish, and all surrounded by the pale gray-green shadows of monsters, varying, fading, coming clear, darting down and sheering away, the same inevitable tragedy happened. This virgin sea was alive with fish, and on this day few that I saw weighed under a hundred pounds. The dolphin and yellowtail were the largest I had ever seen, larger than I had ever imagined they could grow. How perfectly at home all these fish! It was indeed the most perfect illustration of the survival of the fittest. I had a dolphin like a speckled bar of gold; and all of a sudden he seemed to be absorbed by one of the gray moving things. What happened to the dozen or more tuna I hooked could only be guessed at, as they sounded deep.

Probably I, as an angler, was expecting and hoping too much. No fisherman had ever yet succeeded in catching the great game fish of the tropic seas. So far as I know, there had never been any other anglers try it. Small fish, of course, can be hooked and dragged in; but these were not what I wanted. The privilege of seeing them swarm in the translucent water, exquisitely colored

DOLPHIN, 51½ POUNDS. WORLD RECORD SO FAR AS KNOWN. CAUGHT BY
ZANE GREY AT GALAPAGOS

PLATE XVI

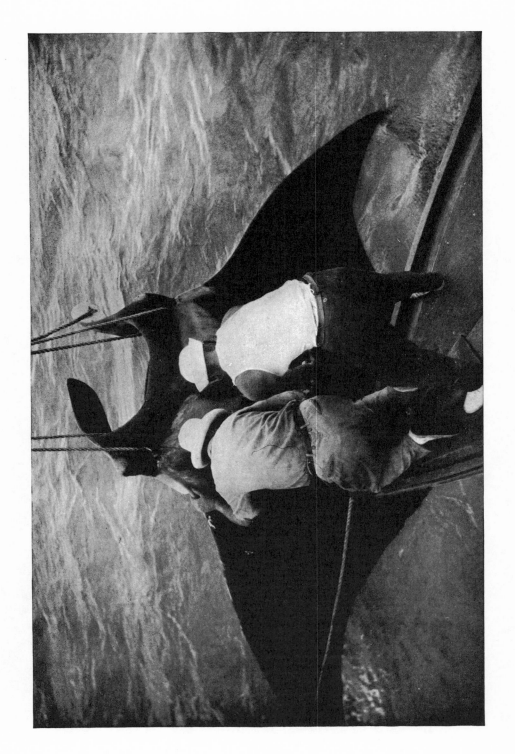

GIANT RAY, OR DEVILFISH, CAUGHT AT GALAPAGOS

PLATE XVII

and sculptured, was something that far exceeded my expectations, and it should have been enough. If only I could have photographed these fish, alive, free, wild in their natural element!

I was disappointed in not seeing a trace of sailfish, swordfish, spearfish, or barracuda, or the rooster-fish supposed by rumor-carrying anglers to infest southern waters. Nor did I see any schools of mullet or sardines.

The sea birds flew far out from the island to do their fishing. My study of the boobie and frigate bird of Alacranes, in the Caribbean Sea, had left me little to learn here. I had forgotten, though, the selfish, thieving nature of this man-of-war pelican. They were falcons on the wing, grander than an eagle in downward flight, or a condor in sailing circles, but they were cowards and robbers. High in the air they soared, some far up in the clouds, round and round for hours, hundreds and thousands of them, waiting for the boobies to return from the sea with a flying-fish in her gullet for her baby. Towards sunset, when the boobies thronged home, the frigate birds dropped down out of the sky and the strife of wild Cocos Island was intensified for our watching eyes. Many a boobie I saw set upon by two, three, and even six of these great-winged sea-hawks, and so pecked and harassed that she soon disgorged her fish, for one of the pursuers to snap up.

I saw several cases where boobies outwitted the larger, swifter birds, and at that by so simple an expedient, I wondered more of them did not have recourse to it. They darted down to alight in the water, where the vicious frigate birds would not go. Every time, however, that a boobie essayed to rise and escape, he was sure to be again beset by foes. One boobie deliberately stayed in the water until the frigate birds flew away. Then she rose and soared toward the looming Bird Rock;

[39]

and I was assured at least one little boobie would get his supper.

The frigate birds do not go into the water. While fishing we entangled our lines with the birds, pulling them down and immersing them. When they got their wings wet they could not rise, let alone fly. Several we caught and put on the deck or gunwale, where they appeared contented until their wings dried. Then they flew away.

These hawks do not appear to be adept at fishing for themselves. They have a long hooked beak and can pick up bits of fish off the surface, but I greatly doubt that they do very well at catching live fish.

They are shorter birds than those of Florida, not so glossy black, and more white-breasted. I observed several with red throats. They have rather short wide tails deeply notched like that of an Everglade kite. The Florida species is a longer, slimmer, more gracefully clean-cut bird, glossy black and silky, with two long single feathers in the tail. The Caribbean species is a much larger bird than either, spreading sometimes eight feet from tip to tip. But anywhere these strange sea birds are beautiful and fascinating to watch. They are a product of the tropic seas.

We spent a day on the beach at Wreck Bay, not the least pleasure of which was in hunting signs that might indicate the place where adventurers had sought buried treasure. No person who ever had the privilege of seeing Cocos Island, and landing on its wild shores, could doubt the stories of buried treasure. It was the ideal pirate island. We found where determined treasure-seekers had dug deep and long. One party had left a large quantity of dynamite there, and no doubt were greatly relieved by its absence while sailing home. To find treasure on Cocos Island I considered a matter of very remote possibility. That, however, did not mitigate the keen exciting lure to try for the Peruvian twelve-million-dollar treasure. It is there, somewhere—gold plate, jewels, coin, in an iron chest, hidden in a vine-covered cave, no doubt, dry and safe and intact for some one to find some day by accident. May the finder be an honest needy fisherman!

A significant proof of the remoteness and isolation of Cocos Island is seen in the names of pirates, sailors, ships, and treasure-seekers, carved in the rocks along the beach. The *Dying Dart* was one striking name of a ship; and surely that belonged to a pirate. Dates as far back as 1817 were clearly decipherable; and there were many so eroded by sea and rain that they were no longer clear. It was a temptation hard to resist—the desire to leave my name there carven in a solid rock of that lonely island. Not that it would be an example of fool's names in public places! I think Cocos Island meant more to me than that.

The sunset of the day we left Cocos Island was the most impressive and beautiful of the many we saw there. There were no golds or roses or pinks. Great masses of cumulus cloud, pearl gray in body, with margins of silver, floated over the mountain; and in the open rifts shone the sky, lavender and mauve, as if reflecting the sun rays from the clouds.

Before the sun set the moon rose, full, blazing white, the grandest moon I had ever seen; and it was moonlight while day still lingered. No darkness came. I could tell by looking at the canyons of the island the difference between shadow and moonlight, but it was not marked. The scene was too beautiful, weird, magnified for speech. To gaze up at the moon, hung in the dark sky, was to be stunned. Moan of surf, the hum of insects, the scream of wild fowl, only intensified the sensations of loneliness and solitude, the meaning of this tropic isle.

We sailed out of the bay and headed to the southwest, out into a moon-blanched sea as light as day, yet softened, shadowed by an invisible and transparent veil.

Cocos Island loomed black, bold, a range of peaks against the star-sown sky, mysterious and aloof, keeping its secrets, and, like its bird life, sufficient unto itself. I was reluctant to go, yet glad. It was one place where I would not have cared to stay long. There are places too primitive for the good of man—too strangely calling to the past ages and their deep instincts. And I watched it fade into the opaque nothingness of the vast Pacific.

The Lonely Desolate Shore of Indefatigable Island, Galapagos

PLATE XVIII

The Shore of Indefatigable Island, Galapagos

PLATE XIX

CHAPTER VI

FACTS are often inimical to romance, but they are very important when it comes to distance. We had been told at Balboa that Cocos Island lay anywhere from one hundred and fifty to three hundred miles off the mainland. As a matter of fact the chart and the log made it over five hundred and forty. The same inaccuracy applied to the distance between Cocos Island and the Galapagos. When we left Cocos the chart showed that we had four hundred and fifty to run.

The wide waste of blue waters appalled me, especially at night, when the moon soared blazing and white, surrounded by pale-green effulgence. Hour after hour the sails flapped, the booms creaked, the dark waters glided by; and yet we seemed never to be getting anywhere.

The solemn days were easier to bear because of the clear white light of day, and the hope of seeing bird or fish life, even if there were none. For two days the ocean appeared barren of life. But how beautiful in its vivid blue, its gentle swell, its solitude and tranquillity!

Then we began to see bonita darting ahead of the bow, and splashes on the distant horizon, and unknown sea birds, and schools of porpoises. Once we ran across the smooth oily track—slick it is called—of a whale that had sounded. I saw a boobie, white as snow, with black-tipped wings. Flying-fish showed occasionally, scattering after they rose.

We ran across a school of dolphin, long and slim, and more agile than the northern species. They leaped often, sometimes lifting lazily and high, and at others shooting out, to cavort in the air, twisting like steel projectiles, and then to hit the water with a sharp splash.

In the afternoon we had the rare good fortune to pass within a few hundred yards of a school of porpoises, small and short and black, feeding on the surface. Boobies were hovering over them, darting down. And big silver-white tuna were smashing the water into the familiar sharp spurts, and leaping high to dive down. This species was neither the yellow-fin or long-fin, so it must have been the blue-fin. R. C. and Bob, Captain Mitchell and Sid and I, all identified this tuna, as well as it could possibly be done, as the blue-fin. We were exceedingly pleased.

When the ship reached a point about two hundred yards behind the porpoises and tuna, and somewhat to their left, they suddenly ceased feeding and began to leap and plunge away from us, charging in almost a solid line, churning the water white. It was so extraordinary and new a spectacle that we loudly exclaimed our delight. For a few moments tuna showed here and there in that splashing formation; then they vanished to give place to porpoises. These kept up the leaping, almost with straight front, for fully a quarter of a mile. Then they slackened their leaps, and slowed down, and sounded. We could only conclude that this mixed school of fishes and porpoises had taken fright at the near approach of the ship.

Our intention had been to strike our first anchorage in the Galapagos Archipelago at Tagus Cove, in Albemarle Sound. But we decided later to head for Conway Bay on Indefatigable Island, and altered our course to this end.

The change gave us advantage of the light breeze, and we glided along over a summer sea at eight knots. On all sides above the horizon trade-wind clouds shone pearly white in the bright sunlight. Their regular formation and level bottoms reminded me of the trade-wind clouds over the Gulf Stream. They added not only beauty but comfort to our ride down the Pacific under the tropic skies. The early still morning had been very hot and humid, so that any effort was disagreeable, but at three o'clock, with the breeze freshening, the air grew delightful, even cool, and sailing was most enjoyable. I seemed to lose track of days. The immensity of trackless lonely seas lay behind me.

The night of the full moon I remained on deck late, unable to resist the enchantment of the marvelous silver orb and the immense white track it cast upon the radiant sea. All seemed magnified—the starry dome above, the wide circle of the horizon, the dark ocean with its moon-whitened road, broad as a great river. There was a dancing ripple on the water. This watching and feeling of mine augmented the sense of immeasurable distance.

We expected to sight the first island of the Galapagos group sometime in the early hours of the morning. Navigation had been perplexing, owing to inaccuracies of the chart, and the influence of tides and currents. The first twenty-four hours out from Cocos Island we drifted over twoscore miles off our course; the next day ten; and the following, when our navigators made allowance for this drift, there was no perceptible change at all.

I went on deck at three o'clock in the morning. The moon had paled and diminished somewhat, and was sloping away from the zenith. Broken trade-wind clouds covered the sky; and low down on the horizon they were dark and vague.

I spent hours on the bow with the lookout, peering through the opaque silvery gloom, over the black waters, to sight land. Once I saw a huge bird, bow-winged, silent and uncanny, that sailed across our ship, silhouetted against the moon. It reminded me of the albatross of the Ancient Mariner.

Dawn came, gray, shadowy, with a freshening cool breeze. The trade-wind clouds in the east took on a tinge of rose. The horizon brightened. Red and gold burned on the level bottoms of the clouds. And when the fiery disk of the sun peeped up from the underworld I realized that I was gazing at my first sunrise on the equator. The difference seemed too great for me to grasp.

Shortly after sunrise I sighted the land that the mate had seen from the masthead. A dim low mound, as illusive and vague as a cloud! But it grew. My sensations were indescribable. I could only gaze until my eyes dimmed. Galapagos!

The blur on the horizon lifted, spread, darkened, took shape, and at last merged into an island with a high peak, a range of hills to the south, and to the north an endlessly long slope, going down into the sea. An hour later we identified it as Marchena (Bindlowe) and another to the west as Pinta (Abingdon).

When we approached close enough to Marchena to distinguish color and nature I saw it to be a desert island, iron-hued and gray, ghastly, stark, barren, yet somehow beautiful. How incredible the change between Cocos and Marchena, only a little over four hundred miles apart! It recalled to me long ridges of Arizona desert land, and there was a thrill in the familiarity. This tropic island excited emotions of awe and grandeur. Forbidding and inhospitable, it seemed to warn the mariner to pass on down the lanes of the sea.

Beyond Marchena a low dark rambling cloud above the horizon soon took on the stability of land. Another island of the Galapagos Archipelago! We were uncertain as to which island this was, but inclined to the opinion that it was San Salvador (James I).

While nearing the coast of Marchena I saw a ragged line of white surf along the bronze shore, and high on the dark slopes patches and squares of pale green verdure, probably brush and cactus.

A most welcome surprise was the delightful cool weather and fresh exhilarating air. While approaching the equator we had expected it to be torrid. The sea was violet, ruffled with whitecaps.

Darwin's *Voyage of H. M. S. "Beagle"* has for many years been one of my favorite books; and became so long before I entertained the remotest dream of ever visiting the Galapagos. This great naturalist's account of his visit to the islands was as fascinating to me as fiction, or *Robinson Crusoe;* and through it I came to learn considerably about this archipelago. Then later Mr. Beebe's beautiful volume, *Galapagos, World's End,* published in 1924, revived and added to my interest. Both are scientific books, and as absorbing to me as narrative of adventure. The latter volume includes a chapter on Galapagos fishing, by Mr. McKay, a scientist who was a member of the Beebe expedition, and the information it imparted had some little bearing on my own venturesome expedition.

There are ten or more islands in the Galapagos Archipelago, five of them large; and geologically they are of recent (geographically) volcanic origin. Darwin records no less than two thousand craters on the islands. One of these was smoking in 1830, during his visit.

The islands lay on the equator and are washed by the Humbolt current, a strange river of the sea similar to the Gulf Stream. It runs up out of the Antarctic Ocean, along the South American shore, and somewhere off Peru swings west to touch the Galapagos. It has a temperature fifteen to twenty degrees colder than the surrounding hot ocean waters. Between the Galapagos Islands are channels from one to twenty miles wide through which set strong currents, running sometimes two and a half knots an hour. These currents and the depth of water account partially for the isolation and independence of various species of plants and living creatures.

The early Spaniards called these islands Las Islas Encantadas (The Enchanted Isles). Later Spaniards called them Islands of the Tortoises; and through succeeding generations, for hundreds of years, they have been given new names. The romance of pirates and buried treasure clings round them as of old, and probably will do so for all time.

The Galapagos were discovered in 1535 by Berlanga, who was on his way to Peru and, through absence of wind and the prevalence of strong currents, drifted far out of his course and eventually sighted unknown peaks. These were the volcanoes of the Galapagos group. The journals of all visitors to these islands, particularly those of the buccaneers, attest to their inhospitable and desert nature.

On Tuesday, February 10, 1925, at 1.05 o'clock in the afternoon the *Fisherman* crossed the equator, and whistled in celebration of the event.

We were headed straight for Santa Cruz (Indefati-

MARINE IGUANA, RARE LIZARD OF THE SEA (Plates xx to xxv)

(Ferocious-looking but tame and harmless, some are beautifully colored, with jewel eyes, and grow to a length of four feet.)

PLATE XX

PLATE XXI

Plate XXII

PLATE XXIII

Plate xxiv

PLATE XXV

gable) and in sight were San Salvador, Marchena, Pinta, and Isabella, all long-sweeping mountainous islands, with gradual slopes leading from the heights down to the sea. They presented an inspiring spectacle. At forty miles Santa Cruz showed a horizon line of many leagues, a grim drab backbone of the earth protruding out of the azure sea, as if to proclaim it was not wholly buried in this vast Pacific.

On the moment I sighted a beautiful bird, about the size of a tern, white in color, with two very long delicate feathers that must have served as a tail. Then I saw a giant ray, some fifteen feet across its black triangular body, moving slowly, the tips of its wide wings curling up as it swam on the surface. Next the sharp high black dorsal fin of an orca cut the surface, and after that several small brown porpoises broke water.

We were within ten miles of San Salvador. Huge white cumulus clouds hid the peaks; and the point of land that extended far out into the sea was as hazy and smoky as any desert I had ever seen. Perhaps my most profound sensation was one of amaze at the enormous size and grandeur of these islands.

The nearer we approached Santa Cruz the more we realized that it could not be appreciated from a great distance. The sea leagues were as deceitful as the open wastes of the desert.

From five miles out the color and lines of the island assumed properties that could be defined. Both east and west ends, perhaps thirty miles apart, sloped up from the sea level in a most wonderfully gradual and graceful sweep to the black peaks, against which a mass of pearl and purple cloud had lodged. These slopes were almost without a break in their smooth, exquisitely pale-green contour. Here and there red outcroppings of lava made the color and grace more emphatic by contrast. This green was a low thick brush streaked with dark stems that must have been cactus. White crescent beaches gleamed in the sun; black rough shore lines were encroached upon by green swells breaking to white. Huge rocks, islands in themselves, like immense fortresses, loomed up on all sides.

We ran slowly into Conway Bay, and dropped anchor behind Eden Island, a pyramid-like rock that would have been a mountain in less colossal surroundings.

The *Fisherman* swung round, bow to the breeze, and before my gaze was unfolded a strange and noble scene.

Bold dark islands, large and small, hugely near and dimly far, heaved up out of a sunset sea; and over them rolled mass on mass of amber and purple clouds, brightening to silver toward the west. Strange new world this Galapagos Archipelago! It baffled me. It was nothing like what I had dreamed of myself or imagined from the descriptions of Darwin and Beebe. Yet both these observers had been unusually enthusiastic for scientific men. They, however, did not dwell on the mosaic coloring or the rugged grandeur or the staggering solitude.

Desert and sea together, both of which I knew singly, had combined to magnify each other's peculiar characteristics. I had sailed four thousand miles to fish the virgin seas that embraced these islands. Sight alone of the volcanic slopes and cones, and the purple channels that washed their shores, would have been ample reward for the long journey.

The bigness of the Pacific seemed to lend the atmosphere; and then the strangeness of the equatorial regions invested the land and water, cloud and verdure, with the something I could feel but not grasp.

CHAPTER VII

THE name Indefatigable did not appeal to me, and
the Spanish name Santa Cruz was rather unsatisfactory because I associate it with the well-known
island off the California shore. But after a morning on
this particular island of the Galapagos group I had to
confess the utter felicitousness of the name.

No wonder this island had never been explored! It
was covered with a matted jungle, the density and im-
penetrableness of which I had never seen the equal.
From the ship we calculated that the beautiful green
slope was fully ten miles from sea to mountain peak and
over half a mile high. It looked inviting, alluring. But
near at hand it appeared a formidable and terrible barrier of cactus and thorny brush.

The ground was jagged lava, grown over with a green
covering matted so that it was impossible to see where
to step. Then the mosquitoes and flies that raised up in

clouds, and the torrid heat of midday, added more to the explanation why Indefatigable had never been climbed, and probably never will be.

Little crescents of beach between the outcroppings of black lava were most profitable for exploring. The sand was clean, yellow, almost golden, and it sloped up steeply to the summit of the shore-ridge raised by tempestuous seas, where it met the growth of jungle.

There were strange tracks in the clean sand—tracks that astounded me. The middle track was a wavering shallow rut, on each side of which, fully ten inches apart, were thin tracks not greatly unlike those of a heron. I knew at once that these tracks had been made by a marine iguana, but if I had not expected to find these strange reptiles on the island I would have been sorely puzzled.

I trailed this one a couple of hundred yards, just as I had trailed hermit and ghost crabs on Florida coral beaches, and soon came upon him sunning himself on a ledge of lava. He was about four feet long, in coloration very much like the lava, yet with a slight green-bronze tint. He appeared to be scaly and scalloped, a rather monstrous lizard.

I approached to within six feet before he began to run in a most ludicrous manner, with clumsy wagging motion that was, however, quite swift. But he did not take to the water until actually driven in. He was not so good a swimmer as an alligator, but he managed fairly well.

We found three more during this short walk along the beach, one of which was over four feet long. There was no difficulty in catching one, but it took the main strength of a man to pull him off the lava. He clung so tenaciously with his claws that I wondered what had developed such tremendous power. There did not appear to be any enemies of this iguana. Perhaps that was an inheritance from the distant past when he did have

Yacht "Fisherman," and Storm over Indefatigable Island, Galapagos

PLATE XXVI

GIANT CACTUS OF THE GALAPAGOS. THE JUNGLE OF CACTUS AND BERSEREA, GROWING
OUT OF LAVA, WAS IMPENETRABLE

PLATE XXVII

great fierce enemies. Galapagos was a relic of pre-historic days.

The bright red and gold crabs clinging to the rocks were a source of interest to me, but as they were armed with formidable claws and I had nothing with which to make a capture I let them severely alone.

On the way back to the skiff a fur seal followed the canoe and came up repeatedly within two feet of our outstretched hands, as tame and curious, and certainly as interested as we were. This was my first sight of a live fur seal.

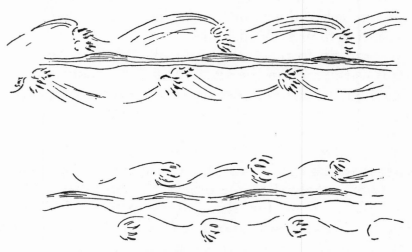

TRACKS OF THE MARINE IGUANA IN THE SAND

The breeze we had hoped for did not spring up, and the heat was torrid. Nevertheless we went out fishing in force, taking the three launches. A few miles from the ship loomed the several huge blocks of lava, islands they might have been, around the rugged shores of which the white seas lunged and crawled, and fell away in waterfalls. On the way out we were interrupted twice by tuna that insisted on attaching themselves to R. C.'s hook. They were of the yellow-fin variety, and about fifty and sixty-five pounds, respectively. I looked for fish, but did not let out my line.

The water was smooth in patches, and again lightly rippled, of a most intensely vivid blue color. Romer and Johnny at once began to hook fish, so fell behind. Turtles basked in the sunshine; rays flapped the tips of their fins like wings in awkward yet efficient swimming motion; small shearwater ducks flitted about us; several great white-and-black boobies riding the sea allowed us almost to run them down before flying; the twinkling, dimpling motion of the water, such as is caused by a school of fish under the surface; crossed our bows. I stood on deck and watched, in the hope that I might espy a sailfish leap or swordfish fins.

We ran up to the yellow and black lava rocks which now towered high in the air. Seals and iguanas lay side by side on the shelves just above the thundering surges. The green billows piled up on the ledges and, turning white, burst into spray.

R. C. interfered with my observations by hooking a pretty hard-fighting fish. It turned out to be another yellow-fin, larger than the others. I remembered that I had come to these far distant seas to fish. Still, even with a bait overboard and a rod in hand I had to look everywhere.

I saw a black-and-white boobie sailing off the summit of the nearest rock, fold his wings, and plunge down like an arrow, to go clear out of sight.

R. C. let out a yell, and I turned to see a beautiful flashing silver cloud of fish go leaping over the blue water. How they made the water roar! Behind them showed vicious splashes, proving that some game fish were in pursuit.

"They're big ballyhoo," declared Bob.

Indeed they were big, and by far the fastest leaping

BOOBIE WITH YOUNG AT TOWER ISLAND, GALAPAGOS

PLATE XXVIII

BABY BOOBIE ON NEST

PLATE XXIX

fish we had ever seen. They almost flew across the water, blazing silver in the sunlight. Then they sounded. I was gazing here and there, hoping to see them again when I had an electrifying strike that almost jerked me back off the seat. My line whizzed out. I heard a cracking splash, but as I was gazing straight into the glare of the sun I could not see. R. C., however, yelled that I had hooked a whale of a dolphin.

We had come round to the windward of the rocks, into a wonderful place where the sea boomed against black walls and seals barked and gulls sailed over us, and green white-fringed channels ran between the islands.

Here I fought and landed the largest dolphin I had ever seen—fifty pounds. It was five feet and a half long, a blunt-headed, arrow-tailed fish with body almost a solid gold color. What a blaze it made in the water! R. C. was so long in photographing the dolphin to his satisfaction that I nearly lost it.

"Say, but I was afraid a shark would get him!" I ejaculated.

"It sure is good to fish where you don't have a million sharks after you," declared R. C.

Bob said he had seen several sharks, two of them hammerheads. But during our fishing around these rocks we were not handicapped in the way that had been so irritating at Cocos Island. I had one more strike, a most strenuous and solid tug on my line, but the hook did not catch.

At five o'clock a little breeze began to fan our heated faces. We turned for the ship, and presently came upon Romer and Johnny in their boat with Captain Mitchell. They reported a most successful afternoon, and showed us tuna, bonita, grouper, and several great cero-mackerel. These last named were very welcome to us, for they are the best of food fish. McKay, in Mr. Beebe's book, mentioned golden-spotted Spanish mackerel. These fish have gold spots and seemed to be identical with the cero-mackerel of the Gulf Stream. According to the boys they exhibited wonderful fighting qualities.

Upon arriving once more at the ship I found myself pretty well exhausted. It had been a busy day, but would have been nothing unusual for me had it not been for the heat. I felt better after a shower-bath, my first in the Humbolt Stream water. It was actually cold, compared to that around Cocos Island.

When I came on deck the sun was setting in magnificent gold and purple splendor. Away to the north a vast bank of salmon-pink cloud shone refulgently. Over the endless green slope of Santa Cruz masses of gray clouds had congregated, and they had encompassed the peaks. Dark veils of rain were hanging from the under edge, making a bar against the violet sky beyond. The *Fisherman* at anchor on an opal sea; the strange entrancing islands all around, varied, beautiful; the soaring of long-tailed frigate birds; the low moan of the surf; and lastly a school of rays, gigantic bat-winged creatures of the sea, flopping along the surface of the tranquil water, showing their kite-shaped white-barred forms and hawk-like heads—all these things thrilled me, revived my joy in one of the wildest and lonesomest places in all the Seven Seas.

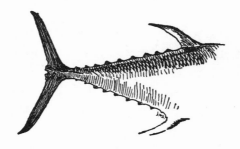

CHAPTER VIII

OTHER hot days contributed to the growing appreciation that the pleasant weather conditions under which we had sailed down into Conway Bay had passed us by. The pitch oozed out of the deck and the rail was too hot to touch. The staterooms were antechambers of the torrid zone. I found a woolen shirt, after the ordeal of putting it on, to be cooler than thin cotton ones. We all burned black. Romer and Johnny might have gone into motion-pictures as savages. In fact, they almost reverted.

Nevertheless, we fished morning and afternoon, made raids on the beach, ate sparingly and drank water copiously, fought the sticky flies by day and the hungry mosquitoes by night, and had a perfectly wonderful time.

I, more noticeably than any of the others, began to grow a little thin. Romer was affected, too, though at the same time he appeared to be growing taller. Sometimes I was exhausted, but I began to stand the heat better than at first. When the sky clouded over, which happened before noon every day, the weather was bearable. At night it was cool on deck. Direct contact with the sun, however, between nine and five, was something to remember. It reminded me that I had always been a sun-worshiper, like an Indian, and that for once in my life I had began to dream of tinkling ice in pitchers of crystal water, and the sleet and snow of New York, which I had always hated. Experience develops. Sometimes I wonder why Ulysses, the Homeric wanderer, did not learn to stay home.

The brush covering of Santa Cruz Island was as impenetrable as a wall, and infinitely more cruel. Rhododendron thickets along Pennsylvania trout streams, mangrove swamps in the Everglades of Florida, manzanita copses in the Tonto Basin of Arizona, have at different times tortured me. The *cholla* cactus on the slopes of Pinacate have turned me back. But I never saw a worse place than the jungle of this particular Galapagos island. No doubt the intense heat supplied the last and most implacable barrier. My explorations were limited to a mile of the coast near where the ship lay at anchor.

On the sea, however, we ranged near and far, as fishermen must range to find fish. Our launches were fast and could cover long distances. Around the small islands and the monument-like rocks we found fish in abundance, with only an occasional shark to harass us, but out in the open channels, in the deep water, where the great game fish, such as sailfish, swordfish, spearfish, should be found, we had not yet had a strike or seen a telltale fin. This was by no means conclusive evidence that these fish did not frequent the Galapagos waters; but if persistent further search met with a like result we would, despite our reluctance, be forced to surrender to that fact.

The needlefish of this latitude appeared to be the same size and shape of those in the Caribbean and along the Florida Keys, but he differed markedly in disposition and likewise in color, being a pearly white. He attacked baits one-third as long as himself, and when hooked showed remarkable fighting qualities. Moreover, he was pugnacious, something new to me. R. C.

Shore Line of Perlos Island. Many of the Trees Were in Blossom, White and Pink

PLATE XXX

Fishing Along Shore of Perlos Island

PLATE XXXI

caught one that was snagged in the side. Bob grasped the leader and unceremoniously jerked the fish out of the water. As it came over the gunwale into the boat it twisted and threshed so violently that I was amazed. Suddenly it snapped at Bob's leg. The long needle jaws opened wide and caught Bob just above the knee. Bob yelled lustily. For a man used to fish all his days this was surprising. Then the way he tore it loose and slammed it down, and the language he used, attested to something indeed very unusual.

"He bit me!" ejaculated Bob, when his volley of abuse ended.

Examination proved that the needlefish had brought blood on both sides of Bob's leg, making slight, but painful wounds.

George Takahashi had a more severe experience than Bob's, and one that caused considerable merriment. We were inshore on Santa Cruz, and after a long climb over the jagged lava, under the hot sun, we went into the water to cool off. George was the only one of us who had worn his bathing suit. The rest of us waded in without removing any clothes. A white sandy beach and crystal green water made a delightful place to bathe. The water was deliciously cool. I simply could not get enough of it. Presently I heard the boys yelling and Takahashi exclaiming, so I joined them to learn what had happened. George's face was a study. He sat on the wet sand, just at the edge of the creeping waves, and he appeared to be trying to embrace all of his anatomy at once.

"Me step on sea porcupine with one foot," said George, with a wry grin. "Then step on another with other foot. Me sit down. Nothin' else to do! An' I sit right on another porcupine. Hurt orful!"

Along these sandy coves between the jutting capes of lava we found the quiet green waters alive with fish. I identified mullet, angel fish, and *revalo*. These latter usually occurred in schools of five or six, and were large fish, up to fifteen or eighteen pounds. They allowed me to wade within ten feet of where they lay, long silvery fish shapes, resembling that of muskalonge or barracuda. They had big staring black eyes, and a black line down the middle of the side. I have caught this same fish in the Gulf of Mexico, and also in the Everglade rivers, where they are called snook. They are game fish and when hooked make a leaping fight.

On Friday, February 13th, I returned from my morning fishing to find that R. C. was nowhere in sight. We do not often fish alone, and when in separate boats usually kept pretty close watch on each other's movements. But this morning R. C. had disappeared off to the south behind Eden Island.

When two o'clock came without any sign of him, I sent Sid with a launch to hunt him up. In an hour or so I sighted both boats coming round the corner of the island, and R. C.'s had a decided list to port. By the aid of a glass I made out a black object lashed to the bow. When the boat reached the ship we saw a huge bat-shaped black creature, with white marking on the back. It was a giant ray fully fifteen feet across. We calculated the weight to be around sixteen hundred pounds.

"Reckon he's a devil-fish, all right," said Bob, "same as we have in the Gulf Stream. But he's a little different some way or other."

R. C. said he had followed three of these giant rays, hoping to photograph one leaping. It was a difficult matter because there did not appear to be any way to tell when the queer animal was going to come out. Finally

Bob threw a lily-iron into one and then a battle ensued which engaged boatman, engineer, and angler for hours.

"I don't know what we'd have done if we'd connected with the largest of the group," said R. C. "He was twenty feet across. This one was the smallest. He towed us for miles, and nearly got away. I hated to kill him, but we can't figure what these fish are unless we catch them."

The giant ray furnishes considerable sport for anglers in the shoal waters of the Everglades. They are har-

pooned and fought on a rope, and sometimes take half a day to subdue. I never approved of the practice, taken strictly as a sport, though I could see the excitement and strenuosity incident to such a capture. On an expedition like ours, however, there is the justification of collecting specimens and data in relation to the strange creatures of the deep; and it is not possible to record very much about them without capture.

The tiny fishes, perhaps, presented more real charm

and pleasure than the large ones. Part of this, no doubt, came from the fact that we could study them alive, in marvelous little natural aquariums on the rough lava.

When the tide was low little pools were left in recesses in the black rocks, floored with white sand and golden and purple seaweed. Here myriads of tiny fish had been left, or, to my way of thinking, had stayed there while the tide went out. Many of these must go nameless, unless I should attempt to classify and name them myself, which I rather hesitated to do. The beauty and wonder of any creature can be admired without stint or doubt, but when it comes to classification, then accuracy must be the ruling passion. That is the vast range between realist and romancer, between the scientific man and the lover of nature. An outdoor wanderer on sea or land has numberless fascinating incidents and facts to record, without undue anxiety about correct Latin terms or unrecorded species. That he leaves to the scientist.

Many of these tiny fish belonged to the angel-fish family, being short and round, almost flat, with wide tails and flowing fins, and colors as wonderful as the rainbow. There were large ones black as coal, with a single white band near the tail; smaller species of chocolate hue, dotted by light spots; and tiny ones of azure blue and golden flecks. These miniature fish were scarcely an inch long, perfectly lovely, and as quick as a flash, yet so tame they would swim close to my waiting hand. I sat for hours, almost, up to my waist, trying to trap these little elusive creatures in hands or net, and except in a few cases, because of their speed, failed signally. Once I scooped in half a dozen out of a school, tiny silvery-green angel fish with black bars. Again I caught a dark velvet-brown one with a red back. The more exquisite ones managed to elude me. Though they would float

with wavy transparent fins straight into my little net, in
the wink of an eye they would be gone.

I caught a number of blowfish, light gray with tracings
of brown, and yellow and gold eyes that protruded in
most uncanny manner. These fish were not averse to
being caught. Tiny sea robins, perfect examples of pro-
tective coloration, lay amid the shell-sand of the pools,
and scarcely took the trouble to move out of the way.
Then there was an infinite variety of slim sharp little
fish, a few inches long, that lay motionless on the sand
until the net approached within a few inches of them.
These reminded me of certain minnows that used to
haunt the sandy bars of a creek much frequented by R. C.
and me when we were boys. We called them pike, but
that was probably far from correct.

The shell-bottom floors of the little pools were alive
with snails and crabs, and strange minute crustaceans,
visible to a watchful eye. I saw a black squid dart under
a shelf, drawing its sharp lobes swiftly out of sight; and
a sea anemone with long golden spurs, like the petals of
a sunflower; and a magenta-colored five-legged starfish-
shaped animal that was at once beautiful and hideous.
The seaweed was large-leaved, amber and gold in color;
and here the tiny angel fish loved to hide. I did not
blame them much. These were forests of enchantment.

During the daytime a school of fifty or more small
sharks played around the ship. They were practically
all the same size, about three feet long, and of the same
species. As we saw no large sharks we grew rather confident there were none, or at least not many. Quite by
accident, however, in the moonlight, we discovered our
mistake. There were a great many ten and twelve-foot
sharks, and one still larger, swimming around the ship
after dark. Even when deep they could be detected by a

phosphorescent glow of the water. Pale shadows, long and wavering, glided to and fro. Occasionally one came to the surface, to disclose beneath our electric flashes a grim grisly fish, fashioned for destruction and hideous in its perfection. They roved around and under the ship, phantoms that left an uneasy sense of their presence, and its meaning. Somebody shot the large one, as he came close to the surface. What pounding smashes of the water! He plunged blindly and struck the ship with a solid thump. Had it been a launch the side surely would have been stove in.

The most beautiful day at Indefatigable Island was one when a west wind blew. It carried away heat and flies, and floated the numerous clouds across the sun, and made the hours only too short.

The sun set on a scale with the surroundings—vast, gorgeous, and austere. A bank of purple cloud, level on the bottom, rounded and rifted above, hung in the west, with a background of pale yellow sky and a horizon of nameless hue. A long low point of rock stood in black and bold silhouette, and almost touching it, though far separated by water, sloped the dim hazed line of Albemarle. The sun, a blazing red ball, sank into the sea between these points of land, giving a singular effect of unreality, of land, water, sky, and fire failing to combine their elements. The vast dome-like bulk of Albemarle sloped up to disappear in the clouds. San Salvador, to the north, lay under a spread scroll of rosy cloud, clearly defined, dark and rugged, with its sentinels of monument rocks rising at each end.

It was such a scene as few fishermen ever beheld in any part of the world; and I absorbed its tremendousness. The solitude of the place seemed terrific. Infinitely more than lonely! Any desert is inhospitable, but a volcanic

In the Fragrant Jungle on Perlos Island

PLATE XXXII

The Rocks at Perlos Island Were Covered with Gray Pelicans

PLATE XXXIII

desert surrounded by deep swift seas of salt water is staggering to the consciousness of civilized man. Ash-heap of the Pacific, some mariner called the Galapagos Archipelago. It is not a dignified description, but it is felicitous.

CHAPTER IX

R. C. and Bob complained that my fish sense, as they termed it, was not operating—that when I did not go out early and stay late, and keep a bait in the water while always watching the sea, it was a pretty good indication that the great game fish were not there. Faced with this evidence, and made to think of its significance, I had to confess that there was something in it.

Swordfish, Marlin, sailfish, tarpon, tuna, barracuda always make their presence known to the alert and experienced fisherman. But on the other hand, fish did not surface in this tropical sea. The schools of small fish stayed down deep. I could not bring myself to believe, however, that the great game fish inhabited these waters and never showed themselves.

"Let's take a long run," suggested R. C.

"That's my idea," added Bob. "It's a cinch we can't ketch any settin' heah thinkin' of Catalina an' Nova Scotia an' Florida."

"We may be here at the wrong season," I said. "Swordfish and sailfish are always on the move."

"We don't see any mullet or anchovies or skipjack," complained Bob. "If we hadn't seen that bunch of ballyhoo I'd swear there wasn't any bait fish heah."

Perhaps we arrived at a pretty accurate estimate of fishing around the Galapagos. Nevertheless it was a splendid proof of our long experience, and the innumerable mistakes we had made, that we did not absolutely trust our judgments, and believed that in the last analysis the way to find out about the fishing was to keep everlastingly at it. Moreover, we taxed our ingenuity to devise untried means to attract fish, and pondered over baits, lures, spoons. None of us took much stock in the artificial baits. Bob, being a Florida fisherman, was partial to the cut bait, which was a long thin strip of fresh fish, cut skillfully, and attached to the hook in such a way that it would troll straight and smooth through the water. For sailfish this was the best bait. But I did not like the cut bait for all kinds of fishing. My favorite was a whole flying-fish or mullet, hooked so that it would troll perfectly. This, of course, was not a suitable bait for the small fish.

The experience of Captain Mitchell, Romer, and Johnny best illustrated the fact that artificial baits were sufficient in these waters. They had great fishing with whatever they happened to put on their hooks. The captain was partial to spoons; Johnny liked the solid metal Catalina minnows; and Romer used tarporenos, squids, jigs, and whatever was nearest at hand. Whenever we happened to look in their direction, with glass or naked eye, we always found one or more of them pumping away on fish. What enormous quantities of tackle they did consume!

Now there was a valuable lesson for me in their experience, for it represented what Galapagos fishing would be at its best, for nine hundred and ninety-nine out of a thousand anglers who might visit the islands. To say the Galapagos fishing was not wonderful would be unfair and untrue. It certainly was great. The fact that it was disappointing to R. C. and me was very little against it. We were always seeking the great game fish, the leapers, the fighters that took hours to subdue; we always dreamed of strange new waters, of huge unconquerable denizens of the deep. But despite this fact I believed we were both singularly appreciative of any kind of fishing, always enthusiastic and keen, and grateful for good luck, philosophical over the bad, and especially trained by long experience to see everything, and learn everlastingly.

"We'll take the big launch and fish together for a change," I decided. "Let's use medium-light tackle, the six-ounce Murphy rods, and twelve-thread lines. And have heavy tackle ready with baits, in case we see a real fish."

It was a beautiful summer morning, with fleecy clouds in the sky and a refreshing breeze. Impossible to believe we were on the equator! I feared my senses had become sort of stultified, and that I could no longer realize where I was or what I saw.

Seals barked at us from the ledges of Eden Island. The water was gently ruffled in some places and glancingly smooth in others. Green turtles showed in unusual numbers. A single frigate bird soared high above the island.

We ran full speed round the corner of Indefatigable and did not wet a line until we were in waters we had not fished before.

I espied a school of tuna on the surface, and stood up on the deck while we circled it. R. C. had a strike long before we got near the dark rippling patch on the water.

"Zowie! Look at my line go," exclaimed R. C. "Now I'll have to wind all of it back."

The task was accomplished eventually, and the tuna, a yellow-fin of forty pounds, was freed. Then we ran

TREE IGUANAS OF PERLOS ISLAND

PLATE XXXIV

A Large Brightly Colored Tree Iguana

PLATE XXXV

on, making a wide turn until we were headed toward San Salvador. In order to cover distance rapidly we were running too fast for trolling. All the same, R. C. kept a bait out and he had one grand strike that made us thrill. But the fish, whatever he was, missed the hook. We circled back over where he had struck, but to no avail.

Close toward San Salvador the numerous rocks and channels looked attractive, and also rather hazardous. As we neared the island, however, I neglected searching the sea for fish, and had eyes only for this marvelous mountain rising so austere and grim. It appeared much higher than Santa Cruz, and infinitely harder, wilder, more rugged and barren. The slopes were red lava, except where the cloud shadows rested, and there they were purple. Patches of green stood out against this stark background. The proportion of verdure appeared very slight, and showed here and there in squares or blocks, very much like fields of green alfalfa in a desert setting. San Salvador seemed a thousand times more forbidding than Santa Cruz. It did not deceive. There was no soft, fresh, green mantle to waylay the sight. We had read that wild dogs and wild burros roamed this island. It did not seem that anything except lizards could exist on such a desolate place.

Some few miles offshore we struck fish, small yellowfin tuna, and in the hope of happening upon a big one we trolled faithfully and worked hard. Sixty-five pounds, however, was the largest, and this one fell to R. C.'s rod. So about the middle of the forenoon we headed northeast across the channel in the direction of the Seymour Islands, great colored monuments of lava that were landmarks even at a long distance.

It took over an hour, with both engines running full speed, to get within distance of these strange islands. The northeast end of Indefatigable (Santa Cruz) was a long low strip of green that ran out interminably into the sea. It must have been level for miles before it showed perceptible slope toward the distant summit of the mountain. This cape of green was what brought out the amazing contrast of the Seymours. They were colossal monuments, one round and sloping, red in color, and the other blunt and square, with precipitous sides, black as coal. They were very high, and the latter at least was insurmountable. Even the sea fowl seemed to shun them. And the green swells beat ceaselessly and resentfully at their iron bases.

In the channel between them and the open water toward Santa Cruz flocks of birds were circling, telltale signs of fish on the surface; and white splashes further attracted our attention. Soon we distinguished blackfish rolling, and giant rays leaping out, flapping their wings. We seemed to be a long time running over to this ground, but at last attained it, and R. C. got his bait out first.

I saw a green flash and R. C. yelled. Smash! It was a churning white strike. How the line whistled off the reel!

"Wahoo," I said, with satisfaction, "and he might be big."

"Nix. It's a tuna," averred R. C., easing on the drag.

"No, that's a wahoo. See, he's on the surface. . . . Now your line is tight and then it's slack. Strange he doesn't leap. Wahoos are great jumpers."

It was indeed a pleasure to fish without the dread certainty of sharks. R. C. soon had his quarry stopped and on the way to the boat. I was afforded no little satisfaction at sight of the long sharp blazing outline of a wahoo. Then, wonderful to see, a whole colony of fish came along with him. They were swimming too deep to permit classification, but I was certain no sharks were among them.

R. C.'s wahoo had to be handled gently, so that he might live when released, and in consequence we did not get the best estimate of his size. But I had no doubt that he was the largest we had caught, something over forty pounds. This was most encouraging.

When I let my bait drift back some yards a short chunky brown fish appeared. He had long saber-like fins. Albacore! When I hooked him he showed the well-known sounding, fighting proclivities of this species. I did not have an easy task bringing him in. In shape he was indeed an albacore, but the warm tints, the gold tones, the mother-of-pearl iridescence belonged to the fish of hot seas.

While I was getting ready again R. C. had a sounding smack at his bait; then a splash and a nodding rod and screeching reel told of another hooked fish.

"Business is shore pickin' up," said Bob, with satisfaction.

From behind us came a heavy sousing splash. I wheeled in time to see a great green boil of foam on the surface.

"That was a ray an' a buster," declared Bob.

Before I could move to get my camera a brown mass loomed up out of the green. The water opened with a roar to let out an enormous black creature, as large as the boat and with wings like a bat. These limber, curved wings waved. I heard the swish, saw the spray fly from them. Then the huge thing flipped clear over, turning uppermost its silver-white underside, and fell back into the water with a tremendous crash. The splashing water went twenty feet high.

"Oh, what a picture!" I cried, coming out of my paralysis, and I dove for my camera.

But this ray did not come up again. Others, however, were leaping around us, on all sides. In the hope of getting a marvelous photograph I stood ready with camera, eyes roving to and fro. Patience is the prime requisite in getting pictures of game or fish. This was an exceedingly wonderful opportunity, which I was not slow to grasp. Bob ran the boat and R. C. trolled. Every little while they would be stopped by a fish, but I kept on watching for a giant ray to leap. There was no way to calculate when and where they might come out. Many leaped too far away. Twice there were leaps close behind me, one of which splashed water on my arm. I stood up in the rocking boat until I was tired, during which time R. C. caught two tuna, one wahoo, three mackerel, one dolphin, and a fifty-pound grouper, almost red in color, truly a remarkable fish.

"Some class to this!" declared R. C., his face beaming.

"I'd say so, if we'd only slam it into a big sailfish," added Bob.

"We ought to be ashamed," I said. "There are millions of fishermen who'd think this the grandest sport. And it *is*. The place is enough."

We ran close under the looming black wall of the great fortress-like island, and out of the blue depths a white flash shone behind my bait. It might not have been a broad shield-shaped fish, for water is deceiving, but it certainly looked like that. I had no time to jerk or do anything but cling to the rod. The fish was swift, and he gathered speed as he went. What was more, he took three hundred yards of brand-new line with him.

"Well! Now look who was here," I ejaculated, as I reeled in the limp line that was left.

"Big tuna," said R. C., complacently.

"No. He didn't sound. He ran off high. Whew! That was a strike."

"Wouldn't surprise me to ketch a buster round these

One of the Beautiful Bays at Perlos, Remarkable for Flocks of Black Cormorants

Plate XXXVI

BLACK CORMORANTS ON THE BEACH OF PERLOS ISLAND

PLATE XXXVII

rocks," declared Bob. "Looks good to me. You ought to have had him on your big tackle."

R. C. took his turn trying to photograph the rays. They kept on leaping all around us, close and far away. I finally saw one come out with a tussle of his flat body, and throw a remora yards into the air. This was the secret of their leaping, to fling the sucking fishes from them. I had seen sharks, sailfish, swordfish leap to get rid of the tenacious little remoras, and now I had the pleasure of watching the giant rays do it.

Then followed several sharp tugs at my bait, a lightning-swift strike, a curling splash, and a tumbling blaze of gold in the air.

"Dolphin!" yelled R. C.

"Now you're shoutin'," verified Bob.

How quickly we responded to the action of a game fish on the surface! This dolphin bounced out as if he were a rubber fish. It was incredible the way he leaped, apparently without long enough time in the water to generate such remarkable energy. He really did not leap, but tumbled up backwards, over and over, sideways and headlong. The only elegance about him was his beauty. His action was that of a bull-terrier with a rat. Part of the time I had a tight line, but mostly it was slack. The sun was shining from behind me down upon this beautiful fish, and the background was the purple sea and those two grand monuments of lava.

I brought him in finally, and let him go unhurt, not wholly sure in my mind that he was smaller than my first dolphin. As he turned over, gaping with wide jaws, his great broad side like the golden shield of Achilles, I experienced a quick feeling of regret, common to me in such moments. Suppose he was exhausted and fell prey to sharks! But he sheered away in a curve, and suddenly shot like a ray of light down into the blue depths.

[73]

"Wasn't he a beauty, R. C.?" I queried. "Seems to me he ought to have a better name than dolphin. Or at least one that would distinguish him from the dolphin beloved by sailors."

On this trip into tropic waters we had seen many of the dolphin so well known to the ancients. It takes a keen eye to detect the difference between a real dolphin and a porpoise, when they are playing on the surface at a distance. Both are mammals, and the dolphin appears to me to be a smaller, slimmer, more graceful creature, lighter in color. The fish dolphin, the golden creature I had just caught and released, should be given a name other than that of the mammal. Its scientific name is *coryphene*.

R. C.'s next catch was the largest mackerel I ever saw, one of the golden-spotted variety that I had at first taken to be cero-mackerel, and it weighed all of twenty-one pounds. Mackerel are usually slim fish, but when they get very heavy they take on breadth that makes them very handsome.

We caught over a dozen fish between the Seymour and Guy Fawkes Islands. When we reached these latter islands the sun was burning gold and red in the clouds above Albemarle, and the afternoon was far spent.

Boobies were plunging down from the cliffs into the water. I never saw one of these incomparable fishers come up without a luckless little fish in his bill. There were half a dozen of the blue-footed species on a ledge of the most easterly of Guy Fawkes Islands, very stolid, stupid, mask-faced birds that stared at us as we went by. I did not see one of them do any fishing. The tide was full, the swells rose white over the ledges where the seals lolled, the iguanas stood high on their short legs with their fringed crowns and backs plainly visible.

I struck a tuna too heavy for the light tackle in hand, and after hard effort, vainly expended, I lost him.

"Well, guess that'll be about all," I remarked, laying aside the rod.

"It's been a nifty day," replied R. C., "and almost squares this Galapagos place with me. One more strike will do me. Bob, cut me a long slim slick bait out of that bonita, and let's troll it along the deep blue water close to the wall, where we always raise a fish."

We did not have far to troll. I was standing when the fun began. A silvery-green gleam upflashing from the depths resolved itself into a fish that all but jerked R. C.'s rod out of his hands.

"Zambesie!" yelled my brother, lustily. "Chase this bird, Bob."

The run that ensued was as magnificent as had been the strike. If we had been prepared for it, with the boat pointed right, we might have saved that fish. As it was he was too fast. He had too much staying power. He took four hundred yards of line off the reel while we were turning the boat and getting up speed after him. Then for a few seconds it looked as though we might stay with him. But no, he was off on another run, and he took the remaining yards of line. Snap! R. C.'s rod whipped straight and a remnant of limp line trailed on the water.

"Short and sweet!" ejaculated R. C., turning to me with fire in his eye. "That *was* a big wahoo."

"It was, you bet, and the third we've hooked," I replied. "Too bad we hadn't the luck to be using heavy tackle."

"He felt like a hundred pounds of lead shot out of a cannon, believe me."

So we had the pleasure of recording at least one great game fish in Galapagos waters.

CHAPTER X

TOWER ISLAND lies northeast of Indefatigable, sixty-four miles distant. We left Conway Bay at five o'clock in the morning and sighted Tower Island about one o'clock.

It rose flat out of the sea, a low blunt island, at first the color of the clouds. Sloping from the south to the north, it appeared to be a rock, rising sheer out of the water, covered with a low mantle of green.

At five miles distance it presented a most remarkable spectacle. Precipitous red cliffs fronted on the north, beaten by swells of green water that heaved out of the sea and moved shoreward with a tremendous regular motion. They piled high and broke to white masses that flew up and crawled back. The shore line was steep and bold, chafed by contending tides, all along the south side to where Darwin Bay opened its narrow mouth. Here the cliffs of lava stood high, red and gray, burned with the fires of past volcanic cataclysm, and stretched inland in the perfect circle of a crater.

The bay was indeed the crater of an extinct volcano,

and the cliffs showed the seams and scars of the ages. Green growths covered the lava ledges. Flocks of sea birds soared like swarms of bees over the island. Conway Bay had the charm of irregular outline, white beaches, picturesque islands, and sentinel rocks, with the vast sweeping green slope of Indefatigable as a background. From the deck of a ship the spectator could not detect the hard evil nature of lava and cactus. But the cliffs of Tower Island stood up darkling and beetling, stark and ghastly in the sunlight, without beauty or charm or vivid color. The crater-sea, with its narrow mouth guarded by jutting teeth of black lava, seemed to possess a stupendous solemnity never meant to be broken by the advent of man. The circling flocks of frigate birds gave the place movement and life, but they should not have been there. They were better suited to the golden-green precipices of Cocos Island. These birds, tame and curious, sailed over the ship, uttering discordant cries. The sunset was shut out by the high walls. Even the booming sea seemed to be excluded. If the waste places of earth and sea had been strikingly exemplified at Indefatigable Island, what were they here? Around these grisly, bird-haunted cliffs hovered the influence of the past ages. How chary nature had been here! Thousands, perhaps millions of years had evolved only a scant growth of green, and swarms of sea fowl, lonely as their lonely cries. But this island was neither land nor rock. It was lava, the iron of the earth, implacable to life, and almost impervious to wind, rain, dew, and the eternal sea. With what sullen surge the swells swept up the steep slopes! The sea realized it had here an element almost as unchangeable and durable as itself.

It took night and darkness, however, to bring out fully the sad, lonely, and terrible nature of Tower Island. The Spaniards of Guayaquil called it Nightmare Island,

[77]

which epithet is not far-fetched. A black circle of gloom surrounded the bay, and from all the shore line came strange sounds, the dismal cries of sea fowl that could be heard in a momentary lull of the almost incessant surf. The ship was indeed encompassed by thundering surges. Far out towards the gateway to the sea they made only faint boom, but for a curved mile of shore line near the ship they were deep, loud, and long, rolling hollow as a muffled bell, roaring up the jagged walls, to crash and thunder back like an avalanche.

The *Fisherman* rocked gently at her anchorage, which proved that only a slight swell was running. I imagined the din a heavy sea would make breaking against these cracked and hollowed walls. But the mournful dirge was indeed loud enough for me. Sleep did not come soon, nor remain steadily when it did come. All night at intervals I heard that incessant roar, the tireless, insatiate sea, the tremendous voice of the deep.

Morning showed Darwin Bay as smooth and bright as a mirror. Everywhere I looked soared wheels of birds, and the air was full of piercing whistles, plaintive notes, hoarse croaks, and resonant cries. At each black point of the gate to the sea, green and white rollers moved majestically to break on the unseen reefs.

We could see the pale-gray lava bottom of the bay under the ship, and the schools of fish that glinted and wavered by. On the bright surface I counted ten shark fins within half a mile of the ship. Not a happy sign for a sea angler! I saw several six-foot fish pass under the hull, sharp-headed, and graceful in line, but too far from me to display detail.

Before breakfast the "go-getters," as the men had nick-named Romer and Johnny, were dropping hooks and baits to the fish beneath us. They did not have to wait

Dolphin Under Water, Swimming Beside the Bow of the Ship

PLATE XXXVIII

for bites. Gray fish with yellow tails, trigger fish with the peculiar spur shape of the dorsal fin, green grouper with brown tracings like scrollwork, and a long heavy golden fish with the form of a bass were added to the lists of the boy fishermen.

R. C. and I in separate boats went out to try our luck. Points of islands, and capes of mainland, where two currents met, have always been attractive fishing grounds for us.

Outside the bay a long slow Pacific swell was running, beautiful to see and easy to navigate. Sharks were riding these swells, just beyond where they curved up and turned green and raced ponderously and majestically to thunder to ruin on the black blocks of lava. I had seen seals and sea-lions ride the waves, and different kinds of fish, but for sharks to do it was new to me. But these were different kinds of sharks. They traveled in schools, which was also strange in my experience, and were long black big-finned fish. As fast as we dropped baits astern we hooked fish, and as fast as we hooked them the sharks took them away from us. Some of these fish were grouper of thirty, forty, and fifty pounds. Fast and heavy, they made it impossible for us to check them, and when we stopped them the sharks got in their work.

We were using strips of fish for bait and it was seldom our hooks could be drifted back far without immediate action. I had strikes from long green fish, quick as lightning, and broad golden-blazing fish as heavy as sea bass, and from other varieties that smashed the water as they hit the bait, but did not show.

We persevered, but it was of no use. Then we ran east along the shore for half a mile, and turned a magnificent promontory that appeared the center of a cloud of sea birds. This was the windward side of the island. How the billows boomed! How grandly they rolled in, swelling to a mountain of green, to burst with booming thunder into white clouds of spray!

The air was thick with birds. We ran along only a couple of hundred feet outside the swells, and soon we were in the midst of millions of black swallows with white-barred tails. Man-of-war birds, boobies, and gulls, and the long-feathered-tailed terns were mixed in with the swallows, but seemed few owing to the overwhelming majority of the latter.

All the time our boats were literally in the midst of swarms of birds, so tame that we might have caught some with our hands. As we did not see any shark fins, we began to fish. R. C. had a magnificent strike from a fish that churned a maelstrom in the water and shot off like a bullet. But the hook did not hold.

An instant later I had the same kind of a strike, and let the fish run a few yards before I hooked him. He was as swift as a flash and a surface fighter. I saw bright green and silver blazes. This fish got slack line on me several times, making me incline to the conviction that I had hooked a wahoo. But I certainly never had hold of a wahoo as heavy as this. I was using heavy tackle and worked my limit on him. He came in stubbornly, then suddenly shot for the boat. I knew what that meant. Reeling frantically, I took up the slack line, and presently saw a flash in the blue water. The next instant I had a perfect view of a huge wahoo, fully six feet long, round as a telegraph pole, barred in silver across his green-purple side. He was sailing right at the boat. Behind him loomed a great long black shadow. I yelled in excitement and anger. But I could not help the poor wahoo. Even as I yelled the middle of his body seemed to be lapped by a black nose. A dark cloud in the water obscured my gaze. I shut down hard on my drag, to save the line, which fortunately broke at once.

[80]

WHITE FRIAR ISLANDS, OFF THE COAST OF MEXICO (Plates xxxix to xlii)
(The rocks were covered with guano and were the home of millions of gannets and boobies.)

PLATE XXXIX

PLATE XL

PLATE XLI

PLATE XLII

"Black shark!" I muttered. "Must be like that Hawaiian man-eater species. That bird was fifteen feet
long."

Soon after that I hooked another wahoo and got him
in. He was about a forty-pounder, yet seemed a minnow
compared with the one I had lost. Presently it developed that I actually could do a little fishing free from
sharks; and I was enjoying myself hugely when I espied
R. C. hauling back on his rod and bending it double.
Whereupon I reeled in my line and we ran over close
to him.

"Hey, have you got the bottom of the ocean, a giant
ray, or what?" I yelled.

"Big tunie," Bob called back. He never said "tuna,"
but always "tunie." "Yellow-fin, I reckon, an' a buster.
He shore put it in high an' left heah!"

R. C. was using the regular sixteen-ounce hickory rod
and twenty-four-thread line, both of which he was pun-
ishing at an alarming rate. The rod described a half
circle, and the tip pointed straight down at the water.
Sometimes it went under. Now and then the fish towed
the boat, but as he fought, for the most part, straight
down, there was little probability of him being a shark.
I waited around on the chance of getting a good picture.
It did not materialize, however, and as I espied several
of the giant rays close by I took to following them.

At some rods distance this huge bird-like marine creature appeared to be a broad mass of dark yellow just
under the surface. Near at hand, however, it took the
shape of an enormous kite. The wide wings had a
curling upward motion, and then a backward motion,
that is characteristic of any fin in swimming. The
ray swam easily, with perfect command of the water, yet
it seemed also to be flying. Looked down upon in the
clear water, he was assuredly a spectacle for an angler.

[81]

Somehow I was reminded of the insect known in certain localities as "deathwatch." The ray sometimes lifted a curling tip out of the water, and rarely both tips at once, showing the silver underside. He must steer with his wings as well as propel himself, for his tail was like a short whip, and certainly could not have served as a rudder.

I tried to photograph him under the surface, a matter which would be easy enough, I concluded, if the light was right; and while I was engaged in this interesting pastime we came upon four other rays, the largest of which amply deserved the name giant. Surely he was eighteen or twenty feet across his back from tip to tip. Part of the time all five of these enormous water bats were visible at once. We were only two hundred yards from where the surges thundered on the lava cliffs. By and by, in my efforts to get right upon them I drove them all down, whereupon I returned to R. C.'s boat.

He was in the act of hauling up the severed head of a tuna that surely would have weighed much over a hundred pounds. R. C. pointed down into the water. Then I stood up to see the wavering forms of sharks. The ocean was full of them, slim, black fish quick in their movements.

"Let's pull the heads off some of these gluttons!" yelled R. C.

Some of these sharks would have weighed over five hundred pounds, but the most of them appeared to be in about the three-hundred class. They swam deep, so that I could not study them effectually.

R. C. hooked one, and a moment later I did likewise. We were both treated to a surprise and a thrill. But that first hard swift run was short. We both pumped our fish up to the boat within plain sight. My boatman grasped the leader, but could not hold it. The shark then began a fight that certainly put it in the game-fish class. I thought of the black-tipped shark of the Gulf Stream, and of what I had read about the mako-shark of New Zealand. This one gave me all I could do, and eventually bit through the leader. We had made some leaders out of a finely coiled many-stranded copper wire that had been given me for experiment.

While rigging up again R. C. ran over close to us and hailed me: "Some shark, this black son-of-a-gun!"

I saw the black-and-white tail of a shark roped to the gunwale of his boat. The tail was a powerful engine for propulsion and the long lower lobe had an offset, almost a notch, that I had not observed in other sharks. Most striking, however, were the very long wide pectoral fins, black above, silver underneath. The shark had a flat wide head, with jaws not very far underhung. He came pretty close to being a fine-looking fish.

So I tried conclusions with another, which happened, unfortunately, to be a very large one. I was using the same kind of tackle as R. C. had. Certainly it was strong enough, for I could lead the shark, hold him, and do almost anything except whip him. I certainly was wringing wet with perspiration before he came to the surface and deluged us with salt water. Sight of him increased my determination on capture. But that was not to be. In something less than an hour he, too, chewed through a copper-wire leader.

Whereupon we put on the last leader in my box, and I stood in the cockpit, bait in hand, waiting to catch my breath and rest a little before casting it to one of the dozen or more long black devils in our wake. Meanwhile R. C. had landed another and was strenuously engaged on a third. We had discovered a new kind of fishing.

At length I felt equal to another battle and cast out

my bait. It sank. Seven great fish curled round it, like trout after a worm. My line went out steadily, then slackened. I saw that the shark which had swallowed my hook had come back for more. He swam alongside for quite a while before I lunged heavily to set the hook.

Then the fun began. It really was not fun, but work under a hot sun, in a bobbing boat, with thundering surf always threateningly near at hand, and most unforgettable of all, with a school of huge black sharks following the one I had on. When I got the double line over the reel I kept it there, and as a consequence had the shark in sight all the time. His comrades glided between him and me, bumped the boat with their tails, and acted in every way to convince a reasonable angler of their dangerous mood. They were undoubtedly man-eating sharks. If R. C. had not been in sight and within call I never would have risked my life in that cockleshell of a launch, amidst a swarm of ravenous wolves of the sea. At length this one, like the other two, broke my leader, demonstrating fully that this especial kind of copper wire was useless for fishing.

R. C. had caught three of these black sharks out of four hooked, using the airplane-wire leader. We agreed that this species of shark was a game fish, and if he had been a jumper would have been second only to swordfish.

"He's a tackle-buster, I'll tell the world," averred Bob.

"Say, it was a sight, all those black devils hanging round under my eyes," said R. C. "I saw big dolphin and yellow-fin tuna swimming with that bunch. Some place to fish! But I never had a moment's comfort."

Unfriendly as appeared the beetling shores of Darwin Bay, there was a quiet little cove, behind a jutting black reef, where crystal green waters and white sand beach afforded welcome respite from the ship.

LEAPING MARLIN SWORDFISH

PLATE XLIII

LAST SLOW HEAVE OF EXHAUSTED MARLIN

PLATE XLIV

Shallow pools left by high tides held imprisoned many-colored little fish; a colony of seals lolled around on the hot sand; black iguanas, soft and shiny as velvet, basked in the sunshine; and thousands of sea birds made the immediate vicinity their home.

The low brush was littered with nests, likewise the jumble of broken lava, and the ragged cliffs standing high above the cove. The air seemed full of sound, the mournful moan of the surf and the cries of birds. White and black gulls, exquisitely beautiful, hopped around on sand and lava, uttering the strangest notes of curiosity and protest at this invasion of their home. They did not take the trouble to get out of our way and could be picked up in the hands. One white gull, flecked with black, had very large, soft, dark eyes, strange indeed to see in so wild a bird. The boobies were as big as geese, and would not leave their nests at our approach, but flapped their wide wonderful wings and uttered dismal honks. One bit my foot so hard that it hurt through my shoe. Boobies and frigate birds nested together; and their nests held eggs, and young birds in all stages of growth. The size of the boobies was particularly striking, and some of them were larger than the man-of-war birds. The most interesting bird there was the male man-of-war species with the bright red pouch on its neck. This sack was small, but when distended by air half hid the bird itself and gave it a most grotesque individuality.

Above and all around, sea birds sailed and wheeled, in rising circular columns that reached very high. The place reeked with a stench almost unbearable. I found many dead and dying birds, mostly half-grown frigate birds. I could find no cause, unless it was starvation. Indeed, starvation seemed to hover over this island, as I had seen it on the Isla de la Muerte in the Caribbean. We saw mocking-birds chasing the black lizards, pecking at them; and we were divided as to a reason for this. Some of us saw it as play, but I thought it had to do with the deadly business of self-preservation. The mocking-birds did not utter a single note for our edification. There was no music, no play, unless the continual sailing of the frigate birds could be called play.

I was roused from sound sleep by a rocking of the ship and the roar of wind. Storm! How the rain lashed through the rigging! I got up to find the time midnight. Hurriedly getting into my clothes, I went out on deck to find R. C. and Captain Sid, and Jess already there, considerably perturbed by the sudden squall that had swooped down upon us. The wind came from off shore and blew hard. We could dimly see the black encircling cliffs and the pale gateway out to open water. All was gray, obscure, weird, and filled with sounds of chafing winds and waters. Our small boats bobbed about and bumped against the ship. If the gale had shifted we would have had to heave the anchor in a hurry and get out to sea, abandoning them. We had an anxious half hour. Then the fury of the storm abated, and our fears subsided with it.

Next morning, under gray lowering clouds, we put out to sea, headed for Perlas Islands, eight hundred and ten miles to the northeast. Nightmare Island looked like a good place to leave. Dark, forbidding, wild!

"Last place on earth!" ejaculated my brother, as we watched the bleak blunt rock of lava settle down into its white-wreathing sea. It was not quite the remotest point from civilization, but it was almost that; and surely as terrible in its solitude and ghastly desolation as the wildest setting of any of Edgar Allan Poe's weird dreams.

To the southwest I could just distinguish the dim outline of Indefatigable, Albemarle, James, and Bindlowe Islands, low and dark above the horizon line. They faded—vanished. From time to time I gazed back at Tower Island. Already it lay flat, a low step above the heaving sea. The moment came when I had a last dim glimpse of it. Then it, too, sank into the Pacific. The Galapagos were gone. Into the sea and the past!

CHAPTER XI

MY intention had been always to have cameras close
at hand on deck, so that we might be quick to
seize an opportunity to snap pictures of whales,
schools of fish, strange birds, or especially anything that
leaped on the surface of the sea.

The second morning out from Tower Island before
breakfast I saw lofty splashes on the horizon, and
watched a while to see if they were repeated. But as
they were not I went down to breakfast. Later when
we were all on the after-deck some one yelled lustily,
"Fish!"

I wheeled in time to see an enormous spout of water
where most likely a whale had plunged back. Darting to
the place where I kept my camera, I found to my dismay
that I had forgotten to fetch it up on deck. Suddenly a
chorus of wondering awe-struck cries filled my ears. I
looked out.

Not far from the ship, gracefully poised in the air,
hung the grandest fish shape that had ever transfixed
my eyes. He was broadside to us and had the contour
of a trout. His color was a resplendent brown flecked
with white spots. His nose was sharp. Curving downward, he hit the water like a five-ton projectile, creating
a thunderous splash, and flinging spray high into the air.

[88]

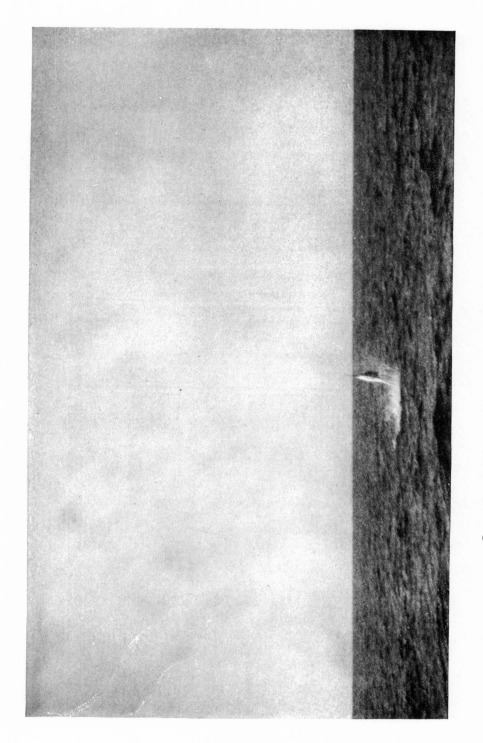

GIANT BLACK MARLIN SWORDFISH SHOWING FAR FROM BOAT

PLATE XLV

Breaking Away of the Giant Black Marlin. Fought by Zane Grey Over Four Hours. This Swordfish Would Have Weighed Between Six and Seven Hundred Pounds

PLATE XLVI

For a second I was stunned. Then released from my paralyzing rapture I plunged down the stairs to my stateroom. It took a moment to locate my camera. As I rushed up with it another and louder chorus of yells and screams acquainted me with the fact that the fish had leaped again.

When I got out on deck I saw the green-white foamy slick where the fish had gone down. As I opened my camera he shot out again, clean and sharp against the sky, his huge round back and wide flukes turned toward me. What magnificent ease and power! Up he soared, twenty, thirty feet and more, and seemed to hang there while he curved his long body. Then head first he dove, sending up a tower of white.

Tingling and thrilling, I waited with camera ready, while I held my breath. The moment passed. He did not come up; and gradually realization and disappointment claimed me. By a few seconds I had missed photographing the greatest exhibition of leaping ever accorded me. It was hard to swallow and I felt almost sick.

There remained, of course, the memory picture, which would never fade. Then I joined the discussion about the appearance, species, and leap of this fish. Everybody had seen the white dots, but no one had observed a white belly and round white spot on the side of the head that would have established the fish as an orca. It was not an orca, because it had a low short dorsal fin. The orca has a dorsal six feet high, stiff and straight as a spike. Blackfish seldom attained a length of thirty feet, and this fellow was longer than that. The only features about him that resembled a whale was his flukes. He might have been some species of long, slim, beautifully shaped whale.

One splendid fact, however, was incontrovertible. This grand fish, whatever his kind, had leaped out of his mysterious element for our edification. I could never slight that privilege. The leaping of fish had always fascinated me. Here had come the very epitome of it. The place and the time were remarkably felicitous for such an event. He had immeasurably enriched my experience of leaping fish.

Later in the day I saw three whales on the surface. Upon drawing up close we identified them as sperm whales, the first I could actually be sure of having seen. They were dark in color, had short stumpy dorsals, and very long blunt heads. It is this enormous head that gives the sperm whale great commercial value. Here are stored the many barrels of sperm oil.

The Pacific Ocean off South America has always been noted as the hunting waters for the sperm whale. That great whaling story, *Moby Dick*, was called to mind. The sperm is one of the most extraordinary of all marine creatures. He is one-third head. He has a ponderous lower jaw, triangular in shape, armed with rows of sharp conical teeth that fit into sockets in the upper jaw. The sperm whale lives upon octopus or squid. This in itself is a tremendously interesting fact. Lastly he is the most dangerous of all the whale family. Many a whaling-ship, with all on board, has been sunk by a harpooned sperm whale.

That night I was awakened by spray blowing in my windows. I closed them. The ship was rolling heavily. A roar of rain sounded on the cabin roof. Hoarse yells came from men on deck. We had run into a squall. I had the comforting assurance that we were away from cliffs and reefs, out in the free ocean. It did not occur to me to feel alarmed.

But more hoarse yells and further roar of rain drew me up the companionway. The pitch darkness outside was accentuated by the compass light. A moment after I stepped out I was drenched. The impact of rain and wind sent me staggering against the cabin. Two men were straining at the wheel. It was then I awoke to something alarming, and ran back to don rubber coat and boots.

The time was twelve-fifteen. I hurried up on deck. Booms and sails were cracking above the roar of rain and lash of sea. In the dim light, through the rain, I saw that one of the men at the wheel was the mate. I was about to yell a query at him when he shouted:

"Steamer close by. Saw her just before squall broke. Too thick now!"

It took a moment for the terrible significance of his words to sink in. Then I went ice cold to my marrow. My mind whirled with wild unfinished thoughts, and an emotion gripped me, the most harrowing I ever experienced. It had an element of stunning amaze. Wind, storm, rain, blackness were to be expected on the sea. But a steamer, invisible out there in the night!

Clutching the rail, I crawled along it, peering out into the furious gloom. How black the sea! Then the black heaving billows were lashed into white. The rain pelted my face. I could not see fifty feet from the ship. I worked round to the leeward side. Here with wind and rain at my back I could see somewhat better. The weird lights of the ship cast a pale glow out upon the water. Above me the black sails and spars, frightful to behold, rocked to and fro with tremendous flapping and banging.

Returning to the wheel, I found Captain Sid there beside the mate. He did not appear greatly concerned.

"Just a squall," he spoke in my ear. "No gale blowing. You should have been with us on the Atlantic, off Hatteras. Sure was hell."

"But the mate saw a steamer close," I returned. "Isn't there danger of collision?"

"Sure there's danger," replied he, gruffly. "We've got to take that chance. We can't see the steamer now and we don't know where she is."

I went to the rail again. The situation seemed appalling. Peering out into the murky darkness, with roar of rain and sea and the banging of the sails around me, I went to the last extremity of feeling before I could again control myself. But I knew my place was out there with the lookout on the bow. I had not been gifted with unusually keen eyes just to use for the selfish sensations of sight. Holding hard to rigging and ropes, I climbed down off the after-deck. The water on the forward deck lashed round my ankles. Action helped to liberate my clamped feelings. The light at the masthead sent a pale gloom down upon me. Gaining the bow, I climbed to a place beside the lookout.

"Did you see the steamer?" I asked.

"No. I went on watch at eight bells, before the squall struck us," he replied. "Pentz had the watch before me. He didn't see any lights."

The mate might have been mistaken. I gathered hope from this and the evident abating of rain and wind. Presently I could make out a dim horizon, a pale space of sky between clouds, and I strained my eyes to pierce the gloom. We sailed out of the storm, and the sky lightened. The moon tried to shine through rifts in the thick clouds. The time came when I made sure there was no steamer in sight. We had passed her in the darkness. Only slowly did the tight cold knot in my breast ease and warm away. Now that the danger was past I became fully conscious of what I had felt. It was not an inspiring intelligence.

The lookout was an able seaman named Brent, the

most experienced of our Nova Scotia crew. He had the wonderful physique of a sailor and the serious face of a student. Like all Nova Scotia fishermen, Brent was religious. He it was who had perched like a fly upon the topmost spar to search the horizon for the Cocos Islands. I remembered how powerfully he had impressed me upon that occasion and subsequent ones. I expressed myself rather feelingly to Brent in regard to the incident of the steamer passing us in the storm.

"Men who go down to the sea in ships must be prepared," he said, simply. He did not say for what, but I divined. The simplicity of his words, the trenchant meaning, struck me deeply. Something in my unconscious attitude had a violent overthrow. I saw the whole incident in a flash of illumination. Men of the open, like sailors or mountaineers, are not immune to fear, and react naturally to the instinct of self-preservation. But they are never terrorized in the presence of death.

I sat there on the bow with Brent until very late in the morning. The ship rushed on, plowing through the black waters, spreading white furrows from her sides. The rain ceased, the clouds broke, the stars gleamed wanly, and the weird moon rode high. It was not possible for me to feel the same by night as by day. I was handicapped by an intense and generic imagination. The mystic night, the perilous sea, the unknown future assumed manifold and abnormal aspects. The *Fisherman* pitched forward, her booms skimming the billows, and recovering with slow, graceful rise she rolled to starboard, then to larboard, in stately motion. The booms creaked, the chains clinked, the ropes rattled in the tackles, the wide dark sails flapped and smacked, and from the depths of the vessel vibrated the beat, beat, beat of the engines.

The sea was indeed not shimmering under a wide and

starry sky, nor did the moon blanch beautiful silvery tracks across the waste of waters. Dark, deceiving, strange, and potent was this Pacific, unmindful of the littleness of man! It performed its mighty task.

On the moment Brent struck the bell and sang out in his deep voice:

"Four bells and all's well!"

Next day the sea was rippling and beautiful, vastly changed. The sun dried the wet sails. Myriads of flying-fish scattered before our bows. Temperature of air and water grew warmer. We had gotten away from the influence of the Humbolt current. I sighted school after school of bonita, feeding on flying-fish. Some of these bonita leaped clear and proved to be shapely, dark-backed, pink-sided fish of about ten pounds weight. Several frigate birds appeared and swooped down over the feeding bonita. The presence of fish was interesting enough, but that of the frigate birds seemed little short of marvelous. They were over three hundred miles from Tower Island, the nearest land. Falcon-like fliers as they were, it was incredible that they should be so far out in the ocean. Frigate birds never alight upon the water. Did they rest upon the wing? Did they fly by night? What marvelous eyesight, what tireless tendons, what mysterious instinct that guided them home to the nest on the lava cliffs!

About halfway between the Galapagos Islands and the Perlas Islands we sighted a gigantic sailfish. I saw his first leap, and I yelled loud enough to startle everybody. He came out again in the graceful sidelong fashion of sailfish, skittering on his tail and just clearing the water. He was fully a half mile from the ship, and notwithstanding such long distance he looked huge. I saw the wide, flapping, sail-like dorsal fin from which he derived his name. He kept jumping faster and longer, while we shouted wildly the number of each leap. On number twelve he turned broadside to us, so that we saw his shape. He had a hump on his back, a further indication of large size. Number fourteen was his best jump and his last. And that number was the record for all the leaping of unhooked sailfish that I have ever seen.

R. C. stoutly declared this fish too big for a sailfish. He looked as if he might weigh close to two hundred. Bob and I, however, positively identified him as a sailfish, at least to our own satisfaction. A little later I saw a larger fish leap five times, but it was too far distant for me to distinguish its shape. Sighting these fish revived our interest in the Perlas Islands, about which we had heard a great deal.

Day after day on the Pacific! Across the equator, out of the torrid zone, north and east across the broad blue waters, into the trade-winds!

What pleasure to sail over a rippling sea, on an even keel, with a fair wind! It was night and storm and an angry ocean, and a careening ship with slapping sails and banging booms, that stirred unrest and fear in me. For that matter, I knew that fear abided for mortals in every mood of the sea, and that this fear existed since the evolution of man and would go on everlastingly. The Persians, the Phœnecians, the Greeks early learned to use the sea as a means of transportation for trade and war. But those beginnings of navigation were fraught with fear, and historic mariners hugged the shore. Vast and incredible changes have come with the centuries, and we now have the thousand-foot steamship. But man never did conquer the grim old sea and never will. It is only necessary to sail the lonely main for a while to realize that. The lure of the sea is some strange magic that makes men love what they fear. The solitude of the desert is more intimate than that of the sea. Death on the shifting barren sands seems less insupportable to the imagination than death out on the boundless ocean, in the awful windy emptiness. Man's bones yearn for the dust.

I was up at five-thirty on the morning of February 19th. The *Fisherman* was driving over a purple ocean, dark and cool, straight toward the beautiful rose of dawn. The east was kindling as with celestial fires. To north and south trains of trade-wind clouds skimmed the horizon, like black sails that had come out of the night. And as the sun burst out of the sea, flaming forth rays of gold and flares of red too dazzling for the gaze of man, the vast circle of glooming water, and the cloud-vaulted dome above, underwent a gorgeous transformation—a quickening, brightening, intensifying of radiant sunrise.

One night about eight o'clock a phenomenon occurred. We ran through a transparent haze or vapor that obscured vision, and out of it into a starry darkness strangely in contrast with a pale translucent opalescent phosphorescent sea. The water seemed almost white, as if a great light were shining under the surface. How unreal and beautiful! The sea was calm, shimmering, overcast by an intangible radiance.

Gradually this pearl-tinted hue of the water darkened, and in an hour the only phosphorescence visible flowed from under the bows.

Head winds drove us off our course and long tacks put us a day, perhaps two days, behind. The days had lost significance for me. Beautiful dark-blue, white-ridged sea! It seemed as endless as the time.

I shall never forget sight of the first steamer after these

PACIFIC SAILFISH (Plates xlvii to lxxii)

(*A new species to anglers, differing from Atlantic sailfish. It grows to large size and enormous length. Very spectacular and gamy. Ranges from Gulf of Tehuantepec to Gulf of California.*)

PLATE XLVII

Plate XLVIII

PLATE XLIX

Plate L

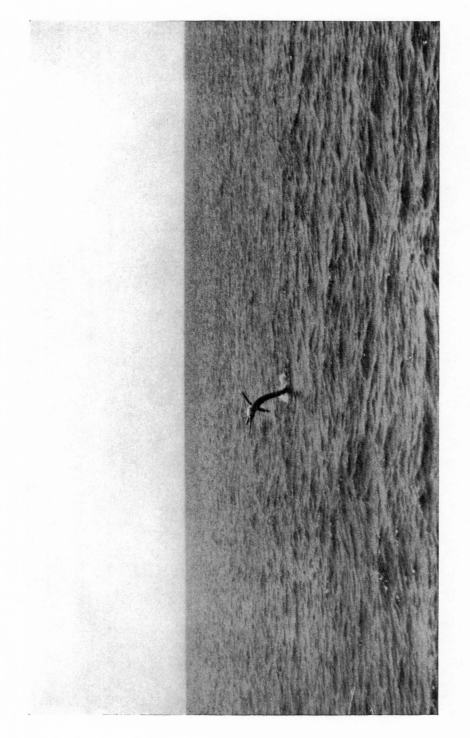

PLATE LI

PLATE LII

PLATE LIII

PLATE LIV

PLATE LV

Plate LVI

PLATE LVII

PLATE LVIII

Plate LIX

PLATE LX

PLATE LXI

PLATE LXII

PLATE LXIII

PLATE LXIV

PLATE LXV

PLATE LXVI

PLATE LXVII

Plate LXVIII

PLATE LXIX

PLATE LXX

PLATE LXXI

PLATE LXXII

lonely weeks on a lonely sea. I saw a column of smoke on the horizon, and after a while the hull of a steamer. Next day another crossed our bow, bound down the South American coast. Then the mainland! Dim dark rugged mountain range—how welcome and thrilling.

The sunset was a pale golden flare, but afterwards a remarkable glow developed. Fan-shaped it rose out of the sea with marvelous streaks of blue and pink, widening toward the zenith. This phenomenon covered the whole western sky, and briefly reaching a glorious climax it faded and died into night.

CHAPTER XII

WITH all due credit to our hard-working navigators, and making generous allowance for the mysterious and baffling currents and the strong head
winds, it must be confessed that the *Fisherman* had to
cover over a thousand miles from the Galapagos to the
Perlas Islands.

Seafaring men claim there is no more exasperating and
difficult bay to enter than Panama Bay. It appeared an
ocean in itself. Buffeting the heavy seas and head winds,
we drove north under engine power, drifting eighteen
miles off our course. Another day, under full sail, we flew
over the sea, losing two points of the compass on one long
tack and four on another. One afternoon we were in
sight of the mainland, somewhere north of the cape, and
the next morning we were a hundred miles south. It was
the wind that held us and the currents that played havoc
with our course.

The last night of that long voyage I lay awake for
hours. At two in the morning I was out on deck, peering
over the dark windy white-fire-capped sea. I saw the
Southern Cross blazing and glorious, high in the heavens
of the south. I saw the Dipper, that the night before had
risen out of the east, with pointers down on the North
Star just above the horizon, at four o'clock in the morning turned upside down away to the west of north, yet

still with those faithful pointers pointing to the North Star in exactly the same position. It was a phenomenon that astounded and baffled me. I watched through that dark hour before dawn, the time which sailors call the graveyard watch. I saw the pale light form in the east. I saw the fire of the Southern Cross fade and die. The first touch of color on the clouds was a beautiful birth. Every instant they seemed a growing and glowing change, mounting by imperceptible degrees to the glorious bursting of the sun above the horizon.

That morning when at last we sighted the low dim league-on-league outline of the Perlas Archipelago it was none too soon for me.

For hours we watched the low land grow, and take on color, and at last separate into distinct islands, large and small. Towards afternoon, wind and sea, as if in reward for all they had made us endure, quieted down to summer zephyr and rippling water. We passed one island and headed in for Pedro Gonzales Island. Gulls and cormorants and pelicans began to appear in large numbers; and the surface of the sea showed the ruffled water made by schools of fish, some of which were tuna. Patches of bait, probably anchovies, dotted the sea, over which circling and diving flocks of birds gladdened our eyes.

"Shore looks like a fishy place!" ejaculated Bob King.

Several times we saw a large fish working in one of these schools of bait.

Presently we ran into a reddening sea. At first I was dumbfounded. Then I remembered reading of just such a rare marine phenomenon, reported by a sea captain from the Indian Ocean. The water grew more strongly red until it was scarlet, the exact color of blood. This more intense streak wound away for miles. How significant that Captain Mitchell shuddered and turned his back! He had been through the Russian campaign in the World War! Everybody on the *Fisherman* was astonished. One of the Nova Scotia sailors thought it was shoal waters. But as I understood the thing it was caused by numberless myriads of animalculæ. Strange indeed that bloody sea! But because of its hue it could hardly be called beautiful.

As we neared Pedro Gonzales and its attendant small islands, we were charmed by the perfume of blossoms and verdure, by the precipitous shores and shady coves, by pale-green mosses and dark-green forest, by slopes covered with exquisite flowering trees of pink, and lastly by long strings of black cormorants skimming the water, and high in the air immense flocks of sailing pelicans.

Romer and Johnny forgot the interminable cruise from the Galapagos, and even before we anchored they pestered me for guns, tackle, boats, trips ashore, and what not.

The *Fisherman* at last came to rest in a beautiful bay, half surrounded by colorful banks and, towards the sea, protected from wind and swell by several islands, rock walled, jungle covered, green and gold and rose in the flush of sunset.

Fisherman's luck means the time and the place and the fish all together! It does not happen very often. Nevertheless, the place where a man fishes can sometimes be all-satisfying, irrespective of any fish. Such was my first day at the Perlas Islands.

We started out in separate boats, R. C. in the large one and I in the smaller, with the intention to troll cut bait and artificial lures after the manner that had been successful in other waters.

First we ran out to sea. The day was perfect, with cool breeze, rippling calm water. Some five or six miles out

R. C. Grey with Three Pacific Sailfish, Caught in One Day—109, 113, 118
Pounds

PLATE LXXIII

R. C. Grey with Particularly Fine Specimen of Sailfish

PLATE LXXIV

we were attracted toward a certain spot by the circling
and diving birds. Upon running over we came upon
a big school of dolphin that immediately began to jump
and play for our pleasure. Some appeared black; the
majority, however, were a mottled slate or gray, slim,
graceful, long, with rather large flukes. We chased them
all over the ocean, trying to catch up with them, but they
always kept just out of good camera range. After a
long chase we gave them up.

It grew tiresome, after some hours, trolling the open
sea without a strike. Not a fin on the smooth water! On
the way in I sighted a red patch that turned out to be a
school of big redsnapper. When we got back near the
islands we had the myriads of birds and the beauty of
foliage to attract and hold the eye.

Gradually R. C. drew ahead and away from me, at last
disappearing around a cliff corner. I passed through a
stream of scarlet water. In fact, nowhere was the water
the color I most associated with game fish. It was muddy,
or red, or thick green, or amber, like that of a lake in
August, and in some places it was so full of spawn and
patches of bait that trolling through it was a waste of
time.

I enjoyed running as close to the islands as was safe,
and most of the time flocks of pelicans and cormorants
almost made the sky dark. The stench from guano was
hard to endure, but I encountered that only to windward.
The full-foliaged pink-blossomed tree so numerous on
the slopes was a continual delight. It was almost as
striking as bougainvilla. There were many large
smooth-barked trees without leaves and some with rough
red bark, like a shell-bark hickory, and others slim,
straight, bare of branches up to the top, looking like
monstrous overgrown weeds. Dark-green velvety car-
pets of moss covered the slopes, and here and there were

vines of brown and yellow. The fragrance was sweet.

At length I really forgot I was fishing, though I still held my rod. When I passed one island there was always another ahead to anticipate with pleasure. In the wide channels and bay the pelicans and cormorants and frigate birds, hundreds and thousands of them, everywhere I looked were sailing high and low, wheeling in thick flocks, stretching out in long graceful strings across the water, plunging down, and diving under.

It pleased me to meet with a new kind of frigate bird—large beautiful species that fared for themselves, instead of robbing other birds. They would sail around over a patch of bait, swoop down close to the water, and poise, then daintily pick a little silver minnow out of a school. Their dexterity made up for the clumsiness of many other frigate birds I had observed. The whole picture of glancing opal sea with its background of colorful islands, of wheeling birds, and the white splashes where they dove, and then far in the distance the dim magnificent outline of the Andes of South America, charmed me to go on fishing where there appeared to be no fish.

A few West Indian negroes lived on Pedro Gonzales island, and we lost no time in scraping acquaintance. The men whom we met were agreeable and willing. They eked out what seemed a miserable existence there, farming a little, and living mostly by the sea. They were pearl fishermen. This season was not good for the diving for pearls, the water being too cold. In March, when the rainy season began, the water grew warm, the nesting birds all left the islands, and the fish came in. It was then the negroes dove for the oyster pearls. One of them, George Samuels by name, a rather intelligent, honest-appearing man, told me he knew of six divers having been devoured by sharks. Whenever sharks came near the diving ground the negro abandoned it as soon as possible. How strange so many people, including fishermen and sailors, have no patience with the theory that sharks kill men! It is not a theory. It is a terrible fact. These sharks were huge in size and could take a man in one bite. Samuels also informed me that the sharks were exceedingly fond of young pelicans. This was a great surprise to me. I had imagined ducks and gulls and other salt-water fowl wholly free of peril from sharks.

Samuels gave us interesting information about big fish. Swordfish were plentiful in these waters, and according to him they were very "cross" and often attacked a boat. He knew of boats having been rammed. Another fish, "three and four yards long, with a beak, and a fin all the way down its back," was also very aggressive. This species must be either a sailfish or a Marlin swordfish. No specimen had ever been taken around the Perlas Islands. At this particular season Samuels assured us the big fish were out at sea.

He guided us, in three boats, round to the windward side of the island. It was very different and infinitely more fascinating, possessing all the colorful foliage, and in addition a wild, rugged, storm-beaten and reef-strung coast, and many times more birds. Countless thousands of these sea fowl dotted the sea and studded the sky. Coves indented the shore line; curved strips of golden beach afforded beautiful contrast to rugged gray cliffs with forest mantles of rich green and pale pink. Suddenly my eye was startled by a perfectly scarlet tree, full-foliaged and sturdy, that stood up above its fellows of green and pink. Then I espied several more. They rose out of the jungle, almost too rare and lovely to be credible.

Among the reefs and rocky islands offshore Samuels directed us to fish. Captain Mitchell was the first angler to meet with luck. He had a battle with a worthy antagonist that turned out to be a big redsnapper. Johnny, who was in the boat with Captain Mitchell, hooked a fish that gave him all he could do to hold it, let alone drag it in. And at about the same time Romer, in my boat, hung on to another. R. C. with Chester, in the third boat, were busy taking motion pictures of the diving, screaming, wheeling sea birds all around us. I left the fishing for the others. This wild coast was too wonderful to miss.

Romer caught his fish, a fine snapper upwards of twenty pounds, while Johnny made little progress with his. We watched near by until the long fight was over and Johnny had taken a fifty-pound amberjack.

We came at length to a place that, the moment my eyes fell upon it, struck me with the singular thrilling appreciation and realization that it must be recorded in my memory book for rare fishing spots. How well they are limned upon my mind! And the charm of living over my experience of them never dies.

The outermost island of this group was a long, low, black ledge absolutely covered with pelicans. Perhaps this rock island was half an acre in extent and rose twenty feet or so above the sea. It marked the end of the reef, and around it the current heaved with swelling power and resonant music. There was a tide-rip that set in from the open sea, and which met the offshore current just around the corner of this island. I could see amber and yellow rock running out some rods, under the green water. Over this submerged ledge the left-hand current poured to meet presently the incoming tide-rip. The result was a foaming maelstrom, and in the boiling water below shone a great crimson patch a hundred feet long and half as wide. Fish! Redsnapper! There were

ZANE GREY FIGHTING WORLD-RECORD SAILFISH

PLATE LXXV

WORLD-RECORD SAILFISH. 135 POUNDS. 10 FT. 1 IN. IN LENGTH

PLATE LXXVI

thousands of them. And when we ran into that current the crimson patch disintegrated and appeared to string out after our boats. The redsnapper followed us. Each angler was playing a fish at the same time, and that, while hundreds of great red-golden fish, hungry and fierce, almost charged the boats. They ran in weight from ten to forty, perhaps fifty pounds. They were gamy, hard-fighting fish, and when first out of the water seemed the most gorgeously flaming creatures I had ever seen come from the sea. While the boys were having such splendid sport I happily remembered that we could use some fresh food fish, and that the natives would also welcome some.

When the swell rolled in, slow and grand, and heaved up on the island to the very feet of the comical pelicans, it made a roar that shook my heart and made me turn fearfully. But it had only expended its force on the rock barrier and had foamed back to slide down that long golden ledge, like a millrace, and mingle with the white foam and green current so beautifully spotted with flashing red fish.

I saw one great amberjack, between seventy-five and a hundred pounds, strike at Romer's spoon and miss it. I saw a huge silver shield-shaped fish that must go nameless. There are myriads of small green-colored yellow-barred fish, very shy and swift. I caught a gleam of a golden dolphin.

Over our heads, while the anglers trolled and struck and pulled, and the boatmen handled wheels and levers, the screaming wild fowl sailed around and to and fro. The deep, low, melodious roar of the surge was never still. What fascinated me most, as I stood high on the bow, was the millrace current pouring over the amber ledge to meet that incoming tide-rip. The two formed a corner apart from the tranquil sea beyond, a foaming, eddying, dimpling, rippling triangular pool full of red flashing shadows of fish.

It was a wonderful place and I had to force myself to leave it, though I had not laid my hand on a rod. Some privileges should be respected. And as we ran away from that white-wreathed and bird-haunted rock I knew another marvelous fishing place had been added to my gallery of pictures. Such possessions as that are infinitely precious. In the years to come, when perhaps I cannot fish anymore—though imagination halts here—I shall have that gray pelican-dotted rock to recall, and the swell and thundering surge, and golden ledge and swarm of red fish. The places that we cannot return to, if they are enchanting, may not be best beloved, but they are most regretted.

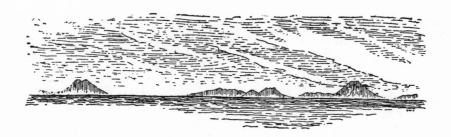

CHAPTER XIII

AN uproarious outburst of laughter on the lower deck led me to investigate.

Romer and George Takahashi appeared to be the center of mirth, and as my son looked the personification of fiendish glee, and on the moment beyond questioning, I turned to George:

"What has he done now?"

"He think he play awful trick on me," replied the Japanese, with his broad grin.

"Tell me about it."

"Romer he want make bet," said George. "He say if I bend back with ten-cent piece on my forehead and funnel in the front of my pants I couldn't drop the ten cents right down in funnel. I no bet, but I say I try, anyhow. So I bend way back. Romer put ten-cent piece over my eyes and yell, 'Get ready.' I say all right. When I just about to duck ten-cent piece off, Romer pour whole pitcher water down funnel into my pants. Scare me! But I no mind. Everybody holler awful loud. Romer like go crazy. They all think big joke, funny trick on me. But they wrong. I keep ten cents. And I say I do that trick all day for ten cents every time."

Everything is relative. It is the way you look at it. Takahashi was shrewd, philosophical, and thrifty. He was not without a keen sense of humor and I often noted how he lent himself to any comic situation, though it were at his own expense. I was bound to confess that I thought he had the better of the boy's trick. But Romer had as much fun out of that as he had the time he contrived to fasten a bucket on Jess Smith's fishing line and make Jess think he had hooked an enormous fish. How mightily Jess had heaved on that submerged bucket! And to land a bucket on a fishing line from a moving boat is no slight task. When Jess's loggy fish came up and Jess saw it and stared, Romer's cup had indeed been full. And it was so in the trick he played on Takahashi.

A day's fishing, too, depends entirely on how you look at it. A fishing trip, long or short, is what a man makes of it. What you get out of life itself is what you give!

We had three kittens on board the *Fisherman*. Two of these, Malty and Nig, had been taken on board at Lunenburg, and the third, a tiny nondescript little cat that I called Checkers, had found a berth with us at Balboa. I asked a native to fetch me a pet, a monkey, tiger cat, iguana, parrot, anything; and the next morning he appeared with a tiny, ragged scrawny starved kitten which I was so sorry for that I paid the enormous price demanded.

Not for several weeks did I give any particular attention to them, though I often saw them playing about the deck in coils of rope. They had all grown furry, plump, and pretty, and divided their time between eating, playing, and fighting. Checkers had a habit of hiding behind something, and when Nig and Malty happened along would jump out unawares upon them, precipitating a battle right there. Malty had a habit of climbing to the rail and sitting there, back to the sea, with tail hanging down, absolutely unconcerned, no matter how the ship rolled. Nig's marked habit was to take possession of any fish immediately it was brought aboard.

Bob King, being a Florida boatman keen on sailfish, took great pains to cut bait and keep the strips with jealous care. I happened to approach him while he was thus engaged, and it appeared that Nig had been stealing his cut bait. Perhaps Bob petted Nig more than any other of the men, but on this occasion he was engaged otherwise:

"You little black son-of-a-gun!" he was saying, severely! "Stealin' my cut bait! Thinkin' I was cuttin' these heah baits for you! Wal, darn your black hide, if I ketch you at it again I'll use *you* for a broadbill swordfish bait. You didn't know little cats made good baits for swordfish, did you? Wal, sir, that's how the Mexicans ketch swordfish. They tie the hook to a cat's tail and float him on a board in front of a swordfish, then pull him off. The cat begins to swim and attracts the swordfish. He waltzes up and swallers the cat, hook an' all. That'll shore be comin' to you, Nig, if you steal any more of my cut bait."

Nig did not seem to be mightily impressed with this direful threat, and made way with one of Bob's choicest strips. The incident served to show me that I had been missing some valuable natural history. Nig, Checkers, and Malty had developed into what one of our sailors called "ship cats." This same sailor had paid the *Fisherman* the highest compliment possible for a seafaring man by calling her, "Home on the Sea."

The term ship cats was quite unfamiliar to me, and I determined to watch them. At the Perlas Islands, where the native pearl fishermen came on board, and particularly at Balboa, where strangers visited us, these three kittens ran pellmell to hide, and they stayed hidden until the newcomers had gone. The point was that they knew every one of the twenty or more on board the *Fisherman*, and that the instant a stranger appeared they vanished.

It gave me an insight into the peculiar isolation and intimacy of life on shipboard.

We hired a couple of pearl fishermen to accompany us, one on each boat, to the waters most frequented by swordfish. But we were not rewarded by even sight of a fin. The warm rainy season was the time for these surface fish. At length we got several miles out to sea, off the first island of the group, and there we raised a number of sharks, big, muddy-colored, shovel-nosed brutes that appeared peculiarly shy for sharks. I had a seven-hundred-pounder on for a while and was soundly whipping him when the hook pulled out. R. C. caught one of about four hundred pounds in pretty short order. After this we could not get another bite. When sharks will not take a fresh bait let down to them it is almost a certain sign of their acquaintance with man.

Whereupon we ran in, and around this island, and across the channel to the reefs and ledges off Pedro Gonzales. For some reason I could not fathom, the birds, that had hitherto been there in myriads, had disappeared.

Crevalle, like green-white patches on the water, lay in great schools just outside the tide-rip, and at sight of my boat they made a flurry on the surface and sounded. Inside the edge of the current the wavering schools of redsnapper, like drifting shoals, parted to let the boat go through. Then as we passed they followed us in a long red stream.

Captain Mitchell, using a No. 6 Wilson spoon, which was the most effective lure here, hooked one; and presently when he was drawing it close to the boat I espied a long yellow big-bodied fish coming with it. I thought it was a shark and told the captain to hurry on his snapper. There was no question about the intention of this big yellow fish. It meant to devour the redsnapper, and as I reached over to grasp the leader and haul hard it swooped up into plain view, giving me a shock and a thrill in one. It was an amberjack, and twice as large as any I had ever seen before. As I drew up the captain's snapper this amberjack came to the surface, and I certainly yelled. One hundred and fifty pounds seemed a conservative estimate of its weight. It had a tail over a foot broad, and eyes as large as a teacup. A cavernous mouth gaped to take in the snapper, which I in my excitement, pulled away from the amberjack. Then whirling away, showing a broad amber side bright as a shield, it went down head first.

I decided to rig up heavier tackles, and to run up on R. C. and tell him I had seen an amberjack that would be a great prize and a record. To my surprise I espied R. C.'s boat in the still water behind the long rock, and R. C. fighting a fish that was plainly getting the best of him. We ran over as close as was safe.

"By Jove!" ejaculated Captain Mitchell. "He has a fish there."

"Doesn't strike me like a shark," I replied, studying the wag of R. C.'s hickory rod and a Coxe No. 9 reel. The fish was down deep and giving tremendous jerks. All at once I remembered the amberjack of Sombrero Reef, where R. C. and I had met with many a defeat. This species of game fish will fight hard to get into the coral or rocks. And that appeared to be exactly what R. C.'s amberjack was trying to do now.

"What are you hooked up with?" I called, cheerily, through the megaphone.

"Regular he-buster of a jack," replied Bob. "I seen him hit the spoon. We're shore pinnin' the crêpe on him now."

I watched keenly, not quite convinced by the loquacious Bob. R. C. had fought too many fish in my sight for me not to know exactly what he was doing and what he felt. Here he seemed at a disadvantage. The fish was too heavy to stop and there was not deep enough water to risk letting him run.

"Turn him, R. C., or lose him!" I shouted, forced to the last resource call we used so often.

The amberjack was dragging the boat stern first quite perceptibly toward the rock. R. C.'s line stretched at about an angle of forty-five degrees. The rod, bent double, nodded ominously. I could see that the fish was gaining line and would soon reach the rocky cavern he was bound for. In a few more seconds he got there, too, and anchored himself. R. C., trying strenuously to dislodge him, broke the line.

We brought the boats together and held a council of war. It was one thing to find big fish and entirely another to catch them. Fascinating as was this wonderful place, it certainly put the angler at the mercy of a strong, heavy antagonist. The hook on a No. 6 Wilson spoon was far too small for such fish. But as we had no larger ones with us we were compelled to make these do.

Captain Mitchell's luck at getting strikes again manifested itself. I was standing when a fish hit his spoon. The swirl and smash were certainly proof of a game fish, but I was not able to say that it was an amberjack. After the first few runs, however, and subsequent jerkings on the rod, I assured Captain Mitchell he had a jack.

"Feels like a whale," replied the captain.

We worked the fish away from the rock, out into the deep water, and there after half an hour of hard work Mitchell brought it to gaff. It was a magnificent specimen of amberjack, weighing eighty-two and a half pounds. The largest I ever caught at Long Key was sixty-nine pounds; the largest I ever saw was eighty-four, and the largest I ever heard of being taken was ninety-

Yacht "Fisherman" Anchored in Zihuatenejo Bay

PLATE LXXVII

Primitive Houses of Natives. Zihuatenejo Has Changed Little Since Cortez Landed There Hundreds of Years Ago to Capture Slaves

PLATE LXXVIII

three. I was perfectly satisfied that there were amberjack here almost twice the size of these.

We went on trolling. It was my luck to hook an enormous redsnapper that I could not handle in short space and time, any better than had R. C. handled his amberjack. I was afraid of breaking the spoon, and did not risk it when I should have done so. The result was that the fish got in the rocks. The bottom must have been a broken jumble of rocks, full of cracks and crannies. The best places to fish, of course, all have at least one bad feature, and sometimes more than that.

Captain Mitchell and I alternated in the catching of redsnapper, as well as losing them. I hooked one that made a fast long run, compelling us to chase him, and then gave me a battle that tested both strength and wind. It was necessary to whip these fish quickly or lose them. When this one came up, finally, a huge red glistening shape, I thought I had never seen a more superb fish. When the boatman drew him out of the water his color changed to gold, vivid, rich, beautiful, and this fact with his enormous size and similarity in shape to a bass, made him a most remarkable fish to catch. He weighed sixty pounds. I was convinced that these redsnappers ran over a hundred pounds in weight, and believed that the catching of such a fish on a rod was something which had never been done.

We learned later that fishing parties from Colon and Balboa came out to the Perlas Islands and caught tons of redsnappers and amberjack. But they fished at night with hand lines, and of course that put such achievement out of the pale of angling.

We made a day of it off the end of Pedro Gonzales Island, and it was at once exciting, thrilling, and exasperating. I had two fights with the giant amberjack, both of which fish lived to fight another day. R. C. had some more bad luck. Captain Mitchell found what it was to have game fish go to the bottom and refuse to be dislodged. When at last the two boats came together again, and the boatmen had exchanged picturesque and profane language, R. C. summed up the situation in a few terse words:

"Great place! They cleaned us out!"

CHAPTER XIV

THE day following we started on our long seven-teen-hundred mile sail to our next harbor, Zihua-tanejo, State of Guerrero, Mexico.

We had a fine breeze out of Panama Bay, and passed by many beautiful tropic islands in green review. That night the moon in its first quarter soared white above the lofty spars. Next morning we were running under a fair wind parallel with the dim mountainous coast.

During the afternoon the wind fell and the sea became smooth. We saw schools of blackfish, the huge, clumsy, bottle-nosed species, and a number of whales, and to-wards sunset leaping sailfish. One of these, which I sighted, did not leap, but swam close to the ship with its sickle-shaped tail out of the water. It was a dark color, almost black, close to nine feet long, had a short beak, and did not show its sail. We saw several that leaped half a dozen times, and their presence occasioned much lively speculation among us.

Early after dark a sudden heavy breeze overtook us and drove the ship racing over the white-capped moon-blanched sea. It was my first opportunity to find out what the *Fisherman* could do. With the great dark sails bent and full, the even gliding motion, the absolute silence except for the steady wash of water, the ship settled down to twelve knots an hour. Under such conditions all her good points showed to wonderful advantage. I remained on deck a long while, fascinated by the shadows of the huge sails, the swift, easy, gliding motion, the moonlight on the sea, and the black peaks on shore.

Morning disclosed a horizon banked high with creamy white clouds, a rosy sunrise, and a dark level rippling sea. It bade fair to be a day for fish; and I was not disappointed in my expectations. A large school of dolphin passed, breaking water, leaping prodigiously high and far. I made certain that some of these dolphin shot up twenty feet into the air and cleared twice that distance in length. We passed blackfish at a distance, and several groups of small whales. One of these was white and had a blunt crooked head. Twice we sighted broadbill swordfish, both of which occasions were greeted with cheers. I saw an enormous ray clear the water and twist himself, flapping his wings as if he wanted to fly. Numerous snakes swam by the ship, mostly dark brown, with white rings round their tails. Strange purple crabs appeared on the surface, swimming along as if traveling somewhere. I had heard of many snakes being seen close to the Costa Rican shore, but as we were thirty miles out I was surprised. The crabs, both in appearance and in presence, were entirely new to me. Birds were very scarce, limited to a few frigate birds, boobies, and sheerwater ducks.

Another day found us heading into a light northwest wind that together with a current retarded our progress. The sea was dark and ridged, with here and there a whitecap. The wind drove us in closer to shore, enabling us to get a fine view of the jungle slopes, the rugged ranges, and, far beyond, the lofty peaks crowned with white clouds. How grand they looked! One particularly commanded my attention. It headed a coast range that ran abruptly to the sea, and its dark bulk sloped up into angry yellow smoke clouds. League after league of lonely range slanted away into the interior. What wild life, human and animal, must find existence in those tropic jungle-mantled mountains!

A few schools of porpoises rewarded our watchfulness, a sailfish that made twelve leaps, and a lonely sea bird. Not a steamer showed on the horizon all day! Barren waste of waters. No one can appreciate the vastness of the Pacific until he has been lost upon its boundless tranquil expanse. My eyes grew tired of staring over the sea, through the hot, glaring sunshine.

We passed Cape Blanco at sunset. It was well named, with its great white rock standing out in the sea. Step by step the yellow-green ridges rose to the mountain tops. The coast invited exploration and called to adventurers.

Something about the red and gold sunset, and the trains of trade-wind clouds, changing color every second, recalled to mind Cocos Island. I found that this pirate isle was vivid in memory. One day, fishing in what I called Crusoe's Cove, we happened to see at low tide part of a wreck. Upon examination we discovered the long dark outline of a large vessel, and a point of bridge or mast projecting to the level of the surface. In the crystal water this wreck presented a wonderful and fascinating appearance. Different colored fish swam in and out of the dark portals, and sea plants waved in the slow current.

Upon our return to Balboa we reported the wreck to the officer of the port. They had never heard of it and believed it was undoubtedly one of the Spanish galleons sunk by the notorious pirate Morgan.

Romer and Johnny found study tedious and the long days hard to pass. One evening, as we were somewhere off Honduras, they had the radio going. I was invited in, and innocently took the chair Romer waved me to. I had a terrible shock. I felt as if I had been jabbed with a sharp hot instrument. Leaping up, I found Romer convulsed with glee, and the others present finding it desperately hard to restrain mirth. Romer had fixed up some kind of a battery under the chair, so that when I sat down I had received full benefit of a sharp electric current.

At that moment George Takahashi came in with his usual kindly grin, and he said:

"Hear 'um music? Oh, that fine!"

"Sit there, George," said Romer, very solicitously for him. "You can hear better."

Whereupon Takahashi promptly took the seat indicated. Everybody waited in a state of suspense, particularly myself. I expected to see him leap spasmodically into the air. But he did nothing of the kind. He sat there very complacently. Romer was working the battery for all it was worth, but it did not seem to reach George. The expression on Romer's face became something delightful to see.

"Awful nice music," said George, sitting back in the chair. "Pittsburgh, you say? That wonderful! Way out here?"

"Get up. Let me see what's wrong with the darned thing," said Romer, disgustedly, and as George slid out of the seat Romer took it. He jumped as if he had been shot, and fairly leaped free of the contact. We all roared, and when the merriment subsided George looked at Romer and said:

"You think you play trick all time on me. But I smart. I put pad in my pants."

Friday, March 6th, a wind came up. We gradually sailed offshore out of sight of land. During the day the wind lulled somewhat and the sea went down. Then about three o'clock somebody sighted whales. We all ran to the bow.

In a very short time we ran into a school of finback whales, eight or ten in number, accompanied by a great number of dolphin. Flocks of sheerwater ducks were flying about. To our amaze and joy both whales and dolphins turned to go with the ship. The dolphin massed close on each side of the bow, close as fence pickets, flashing up and down, showing their silver flecks, and the whales crossed our bow and stern. Three of them sounded quite close to the ship, lifting their enormous flukes high in the air, eliciting shouts of delight from all. We saw six altogether perform this very beautiful and majestic action. I was keen to photograph a dolphin or whale leaping clear, but they contented themselves with merely breaking the surface. After a few moments the whales left us, but the dolphin came with us for fully half an hour, as tame and playful as kittens.

Towards sunset the wind freshened, and increased until it was blowing half a gale. Night came with a clear sky and white moon. A heavy swell rose with the wind. We changed the course of the ship slightly so to have full benefit of a two-knot current, the heavy wind, and a following sea. Then the *Fisherman* showed that she had been built to sail.

I leaned over the bow for a long time, looking up and back at the vast curved sails, through which the moon shone, and down at the roaring creamy caldron that rolled away from the ship. A seething, boiling, hissing, roaring acre of white foam spread over the dark moon-glinted waters. How swiftly we glided on! I was fascinated at the tremendous tumult, at the slow steady rise of the bow, high and higher, until I felt lifted aloft. Then she went down, not with a pitch, but in slow glide, into the black hollows.

From the stern the effect of sails and motion, of the tumultuous sea, was even more striking. Immense swells raced the ship, waving up, heaving, reaching her and climbing level with the rail, only to lift her gracefully and pass on with sullen hollow defeated roar. Far out over the dark rough waters gleams of silver rose and spread and vanished. The track of the moon gleamed resplendent, far as eye could see. The ship seemed instinct with life and spirit, as it was marked with almost spectral beauty. The great sails held her steady as a rock. She rose easily and fell, but there was no lateral motion; and all the time she was rushing on. The engines were dead. There was no sound on the ship. But all around the old ocean roared and crashed, and the wind whistled by. Almost I lost my fear of the sea, the night was so soft and balmy, the moon-lit heaven so lovely, the wide waste of waves so grand and rhythmic.

The coast of San Salvador presented a weird and forbidding aspect—a long, low, dim, irregular horizon, peaked here and there with lofty cone-shaped volcanoes. The sea and shore seemed obscure in pale smoke, and in places darker columns of smoke rose to be lost in the clouds. All day this strange, inhospitable coast compelled the gaze to return to it, ponderingly. The romance of San Salvador was enhanced perhaps by the purple haze that hung low, guarding its secret.

The wind failed us, and again we had occasion for grateful appreciation of the engines. The sun glared down hot, boiling the tar and rosin from the deck. Dolphin surrounded the bow and played there for hours. An occasional sailfish leaped tantalizingly. Once we

MAIN STREET, ZIHUATENEJO

PLATE LXXIX

THE BELLE OF ZIHUATENEJO

PLATE LXXX

saw a huge Marlin swordfish quite close to the ship— the first we could be absolutely sure of identification on this trip. Sight of the great sickle tail gave me a thrill. I could only guess what it gave R. C. and Captain Sid, who are as keen after Marlin as I am after broadbill swordfish.

The sunset was dull gold-red, an angry flare, soon dying. Later the afterglow came out with exquisite shades of rose, pink, topaz, lilac.

When darkness finally settled down we were fascinated by sight of an active volcano, San Salvador itself, according to our chart. A red glow suffused the sky, flared brighter, only to die. Then an irregular spot of fire burned out of the blackness. Clouds of steam rose above it and gradually obscured it. The black horizon lay blank for a long time, until at length again the red pin-point pierced the gloom, grew and spread, flared up in dark angry crimson flame.

From far out on the sea at night the light from a lofty volcano seemed a beautiful disturbing spectacle. Earth, air, water, fire—the elements of the sphere on which we are so helplessly and ignorantly bound—can never be trusted. Nature is pitiless. She wears on through the ages, inscrutable and inevitable. Volcanoes are necessary to the proper balance of forces inside the earth. But to see one blaze and smoke through the darkness is confounding to the soul. A fisherman of the temperate zones is nothing if not contemplative. He loves the hills and streams, the great rivers and the gray old seas. Creatures that swim and fly and graze are his especial objects of devotion. The black storm, the conflicting tide, the thunder on the mountain top, the wind in the forest, are all a part of his experience. And he grows in time to regard all with tranquillity, with the simplicity of the Indian, to whom all physical things are intimate.

But to him red volcanoes, steaming, smoking, glowing, are rare, staggering, and conducive to a yearning for the known waters near home.

Farther north the coast line mounted higher and higher in heaving range and towering peak. Tecana, a volcano on the border between Guatemala and Mexico, was fourteen thousand feet high, a lone sentinel, a symmetrical cone that stood grandly up in the sky.

As we sailed north day after day, through the mild sweet summer nights, moonlit and lonely, the temperature gradually cooled. And what was most welcome was the increasing signs of fish life on the sea. Sight of three broadbill swordfish, five great rays, and the leaping of sailfish revived anew our eager angling proclivities, lulled almost into oblivion by the endless leagues of the barren Pacific.

One thousand miles from the Perlas Islands! And that day the ocean was a dark-blue rippling expanse of majestic swells, so long and so sloping that the climb of the ship was a slow, easy swing aloft, and the descent an exhilarating movement of delight.

We saw twelve sailfish up to noon, and then no more. The day was scorchingly hot, a reminder of the Galapagos. In the morning a boobie, gray and white and somewhat bedraggled, alighted on the end of the bowsprit, and remained there until he began to excite our interest. Finally he tucked his head under his wing and went to sleep. The rise and fall of the bowsprit was tremendous, and how that lonesome sea bird kept his balance was a mystery to me.

"Reckon he lives up heah a ways an' thinks he might as well ride," was Bob King's comment.

Everybody had something to say about our passenger.

To me the circumstance grew profoundly interesting. After a time the boobie awakened, ruffled his feathers, preened himself, changed his position, but he did not fly. He became a fixture. He had attached himself to the good ship *Fisherman*. Six hours I know of he kept his perch on that pitching bowsprit. I made many conjectures as to the reason for his riding so far with us, and the only one I believed worth recording here was that he had a companionable feeling for the moving ship. Wild birds sometimes show surprising desire for strange company. No doubt this particular boobie often had a ride on a sailing vessel. Sometime late in the afternoon, when we had all tired of watching him, and the glistening, heaving monotonous blue sea, he took flight and left us.

We had expected to encounter a gale off the Gulf of Tehuantepec, but the first two days were smooth and windless. The sea was like a mirror. We must have been too far offshore for swordfish, but about sunset of the first day we saw two enormous sailfish.

I was eating dinner when yells above brought me up posthaste. The mate pointed over the port side. Close to the ship, then, I espied the largest sail fin I had ever seen. It looked over two feet high and several wide. A long sickle-shaped tail fin also showed, and there was fully ten feet between tail and sail. I watched this fish until we passed on out of sight.

Later, just as the afterglow of sunset had begun to brighten the twilight, some one in the stern yelled lustily. Other yells followed. I was at the moment climbing to the bow on the starboard side. I surely made a quick job of it, and diving under the boom I searched the ocean. I heard a heavy souse in the water. Then some hundred yards off and forward a long black fish shot out and up above the horizon line, in a prodigious leap that to one experienced in seeing fish leap was absolutely incredible. He went high, slow and far, and splashed heavily back. Again the water split to let him out to a loftier leap. Everybody, except myself, was shouting now, in divers keys. I recognized the motion, the shape of a sailfish. But the size was unbelievable. I could only gasp. He plunged down, and out again, heavy, slow, limber, flapping his wide scalloped sail. Two more leaps, the last of which was an awkward, tired tumble, and then he disappeared for good.

After I came out of my trance I questioned everyone on the ship, for none had missed this extraordinary performance. Romer was so excited that he argued strenuously as to the size of the fish, the species, and distance from the boat. Bob said at first he thought it was a huge dolphin, and later a Marlin. R. C. and Captain Mitchell saw every leap, fifteen in number.

"The first few beat anything I ever saw," declared my brother. "He went twice as high and far as on his last leaps. You could tell he was getting tired. He was very long, but not thick-bodied for his length. I'd say over three hundred pounds. Some fish, and absolutely he was a sailfish."

Captain Sid was strong in his conviction that it would have weighed five hundred. The sailors, all of whom were Nova Scotia fishermen not prone to exaggeration, testified to the large size of this fish. I hesitated to go on record with my estimate, for I was undoubtedly the most profoundly affected by sight of this great leaping sailfish. I took occasion to speak of the gigantic sailfish in the Indian Ocean, off Madagascar, reaching a length of twenty-five feet, with a weight of two thousand pounds. Romer, who was an attentive listener, said: "Gee! it'd be grand to see one of them jump."

We came at length into what might have been characterized as the zone of turtles. The sea that morning was like glass, with scarcely any perceptible motion. Turtles, as large round as a tub, began to show on the surface, and they increased in numbers as we made headway across the Gulf. They spotted the shimmering circle of sea. Most of them were asleep, but occasionally one was seen that lifted his head to look at the ship. Seldom did one make any effort to swim away. Sometimes we rudely awoke a sleeping turtle by bumping our bow against him.

About noon, when the sun was hottest, we began to see birds standing on the backs of turtles. This occasioned us amusement and activity. Terns and gulls and one boobie made of these oval green backs a resting-place.

In the afternoon shark fins stood out of the placid waters. We recognized at least one kind, a hammerhead. Some of these sharks were black-finned and pretty large in size. Schools of bait ruffled the surface, and occasionally a golden dolphin swam by within sight. Then when the afternoon was hottest the ocean again appeared barren.

On March 11th I looked so intensely and steadily, with such thrilling excitement, that towards sunset my eyes pained and blurred, compelling me to rub them continually.

It was a wonderful day on the ocean. A long slow swell and a gently rippling sea came from the west. The water mirrored the blue of the sky. The *Fisherman* sailed along about five miles offshore from the wild and magnificent Sierra Madre Mountains of Mexico. What singular contrast between these bold black domes and the sky-towering volcanic cones of San Salvador! White beaches of sand curved under a line of green that led up to range over range of foothills, which in turn stepped up to the great black horizon, fringed against the sky.

Before breakfast we sighted seventeen sailfish, which leaped from several to ten times. We were all jubilant. Chester put up the motion-picture camera on the bow, and after breakfast we all assembled there to watch.

From that hour until noon we vied with one another in sighting sailfish, and it vastly pleased me that I carried off the honors.

About noon several whales appeared straight ahead about a mile. They were large and black. They plowed through the sea, puffed, and sounded with wide forked flukes high in the air.

As we sailed on they came up off the port bow, nearly as far away. We watched them sound again. Then, suddenly, with a paralyzing unexpectedness, a majestic and stupendous black whale propelled itself high into the air, poised a few seconds, or seemed to, and then fell back with a crash we plainly heard. The splash was monumental, the white caldron of foam an acre round. We were all struck dumb for a second. Then I dove for my camera. A huge black blunt head stuck up and heaved higher and higher, until two-thirds of the whale was in the air. I snapped my camera. He soused back, making a high wave. Another came out a little way, then slid under. As they did not appear again, I gradually recovered my breath.

These were sperm whales. The enormous heads, fully one-third of the entire length, and the blunt noses were sufficient evidence of this species. I could scarcely believe in my good fortune—that I had actually seen with my own eyes the leaping of the strangest and most terrible creature of the sea, indeed the largest and fiercest of all living beasts. For a whale is a mammal, and a sperm whale, or cachalot, has been recorded by naturalists and whalers to have sunk many ships and crushed many small boats in their massive jaws. Ever since I had read Melville's wonderful story about the White Whale I had longed to see a sperm. The whaling terms, "There she blows," and "There she breaches," were music to me.

A short time after this we sighted an orca, easily recognized by his high black spiked dorsal fin. He was thrashing around in the water, making a whirlpool, just too far for good photography.

We sighted sailfish leaping on the horizon and then far inshore, and off the port side, and again to starboard. Strange to say none of them were close to us, a fact we could not account for. But by the tremendous white splashes and the aid of glasses we identified them perfectly. We always counted the leaps, and the longer one leaped the louder we yelled.

Sailfish number seventy was a giant in size and the breaker of all leaping records. He came out short of a mile from us, in a wagging leap, splashed back, to shoot out swifter and higher. His leaps were so long and high that they took up an appreciable amount of time. Seconds, in fact! He had an infinite variety, and toward the end of his pyrotechnics he leaped out in a curve and dove back as slick as a seal. In all he leaped twenty-one times. After that another big one displayed himself in nine splendid jumps. The last two sailfish swam along the surface with sails spread, and these swelled the number to seventy-seven.

And that brought us to sunset. Masses of broken clouds lent millions of surfaces to the golden rose and fire. The mountains were lost in lilac haze, the sea was pure gold, the west an indescribable mozaic of vivid hues. Every second the scene changed. We were on an enchanted ship, with the bellying sails purple and gold, gliding on over an opal sea.

[127]

But it transpired that this unforgettable day could be followed by another, richer in experience, and all-satisfying with achievement.

About ten o'clock the next morning, in a smooth, dark, glancing sea, we encountered another and larger school of sperm whales. When first sighted four of this school were spouting a mile off our port bow. I called to the sailor at the wheel to throw the ship over a point or two. The calls and change of course brought everybody up on deck.

I was searching the rippled water with a glass when wondering and awe-struck shouts thrilled me. Looking up quickly, I saw the descent of a magnificent green-and-white geyser, and its smoothing out into a patch of foam. Next my ears were assailed by a sodden crash. I saw a wave move ahead of the white spot.

"*Camera!*" I yelled to Chester, who had darted to his motion-picture machine. I heard the smooth watch-like ticking of the instrument as he wound. "Look sharp everybody!"

With that I leveled my glass at the bulging wave. As I found it, the sea opened to let out a black snout, glistening and huge. Slowly it rose. It was followed by a vast bulk, black, shiny, dripping waterfalls from its sides. Then it pitched down and forward to spread a furrow like that made when a ship is launched. Yells filled my ears, wild cries of delight, excitement, joy, awe, according as each of the beholders of that spectacle felt. Above it all I heard R. C.'s voice. When he had that piercing, stentorian, ringing note, then indeed the moment was soul-stirring. The sight was so grand that I forgot my own camera, but I did not forget to yell at Chester.

"I saw him—right in the finder!" bellowed he.

The sea smoothed out green and flat, only to burst

CHILDREN OF ZIHUATENEJO

PLATE LXXXI

ZANE GREY AND ONE OF THE LITTLE SPANISH GIRLS OF ZIHUATENEJO. THESE CHILDREN WERE WHITE, WITH DELICATE FEATURES, FINE EYES AND HANDS, AND WERE EVIDENTLY DESCENDANTS OF CORTEZ

PLATE LXXXII

again for a black-headed whale to lunge out. The motion was stately, prodigious, so slow that it clamped me with painful suspense. I could see through the glass with most remarkable clearness. The great sperm whale seemed right before my eyes, strange of shape, bright, wet, mottled underneath. He reached the limit of his plunge, almost all of his bulk out, and he rolled over in the air, with one of his fins standing straight up, and the green-white water flying from his flukes. At this instant another whale shot up, much quicker, right in the rear, and the two of them showed more out of the water than in—an unparalleled sight in all my sea roving. They went down into the maelstrom they created, only to lunge into the air again, rising above the horizon, wreathed in white spray, monstrous beasts that seemed incredible. *Again—again—again!* Nine leaps in all, the first being wholly out of the water, and the succeeding ones plunges and lunges, with half and two-thirds of the whales above the sea!

For long we waited with abated breath and strung nerves. But they had sounded. I have no idea how I looked, but R. C. was pale, and Chester's eyes were flashing blue fire. Takahashi sat on the rail below, and at last removing his gaze from the sea he looked up at me with his rare smile. He knew what that spectacle meant to me!

"My goodnish graceness!" he ejaculated. "Awful good luck."

Takahashi's Oriental philosophy never failed to impress me. It was indeed the most exceedingly marvelous luck. Old whale-hunters, those Nantucket and New Bedford and Norwegian whalers, had seen the "breaching," as they called leaping of whales, but I doubt if any anglers save us had ever been so lucky. Moreover, we were indeed the first to photograph leaping whales, let alone the mysterious and rare sperm, that now almost extinct cetacean, that roamer of the abysmal depths, that fierce killer of the octopus.

CHAPTER XV

IT took almost two weeks for the *Fisherman* to reach
Zihuatanejo Bay. We had to lay outside all night,
as it was impossible to see the narrow entrance to the
bay, or even the single black rock that stands about a mile
offshore.

I was up at five o'clock, when the darkness seemed to
be moving away across the ocean, before the gray light
from the east. Magnificent dark mountains loomed
above the dim mystic shore. When daylight came we
found the black rock and then the entrance to the bay.
The sun rose red over the range, flooding a scene of unparalleled beauty and wildness.

Zihuatanejo Bay opened out into a round placid expanse of water, blazing with the gold and red of morning.
The colored slopes ran down to the curved white beach
and the lines of cocoanut palms. It appeared more of a
South Sea atmosphere than even the Cocos Island. We
ran in for a mile and anchored about the center of the bay,
with the white beach stretching on each side of us. Deep
coves marked the extreme ends of the bay, and along the

shore of the left one nestled the primitive dwellings of the
natives—colored houses and shacks of thatched palm,
and whitewashed adobe. Columns of blue smoke rose
lazily upwards. Natives in white patrolled the beach,
watching the ship. The place was exquisitely beautiful,
yet melancholy with something I could not grasp.

While we were putting the launches overboard we
saw seven sailfish leap out beyond the mouth of the bay,
and if it were needed this was enough to rouse us to the
highest pitch of enthusiasm for this out-of-the-way spot.

The officer of the port came out to us in a canoe hollowed out of a tree, and with the Mexican flag tied to
one of the paddles. He was accompanied by Señor del
Toro, a Spanish gentleman, who first called my attention
to the wonderful hunting and fishing possibilities at
Zihuatanejo. After the formalities were over we went
ashore in one of our launches, and when I stepped out
on that wide white strand I thought it no less than the
beach of an island of the Marquesans.

A low wide slope of sand stretching in a curve led up
to a line of tropic habitations. Several huge glossy-green

tent-like trees made great spaces of shade on the sand under which children were playing, women were cooking, men were hewing boats out of logs. The children were beautiful, white-skinned, with great dark Spanish eyes, fine features and hair. I waded through the deep sand of the one street, and enjoyed the most picturesque scene it had ever been my privilege to see. Dogs, parrots, deer, pigs shared the shade with the children. I spent several hours ashore, about which experience I must write again.

I showed pictures of broadbill and Marlin swordfish to the native whom Señor del Toro said knew the game and fish adjacent to Zihuatanejo. He recognized both species, and he described a leaping fish, which he called *Pepe vela*, in a way to assure me that we had been right about the sailfish. But none of these fish had ever been caught in any way.

We anticipated difficulty in getting bait, and surely were right, but at length a native netted a few mullet for us, and we caught several mackerel.

Next morning we were up before daylight and out on the ocean before sunrise. The day was perfect, smooth, clear, balmy. We had to fight the boobies to keep our baits in the water. We trolled out beyond Black Rock, the three boats keeping together. But soon R. C. espied whales and I joined him in chasing them, with the object, of course, of photographing them. They turned out to be four large sperm whales, and they were traveling west, blowing often, sounding occasionally, and affording us an unparalleled opportunity. The under side of the flukes of the largest of these whales was pure white. Often we saw it raised high in the air, sometimes with a black one equally as large. We chased them, and probably approached them closer than was wise, but the temptation for pictures was irresistible. When the four rode the swell abreast, churning great green-white fur-rows, and blowing clouds of white spray into the air, with a whistling bellow that was frightful, they presented a wonderful sight. And when they curved their broad black backs, and raised those tremendous tails, from which waterfalls poured down, it was at once an awe-inspiring and rarely beautiful spectacle. Dolphin played among them, causing them to slap with their tails and raise their heads out and open their jaws. That long, cruelly-armed lower jaw was something sinister to see. Finally we left them and went back to fishing. Captain Mitchell was off some distance to our left.

We kept keen watch for leaping sailfish. Birds were diving, dolphin were jumping, whales were splashing, schools of small fish broke the surface, but we failed to see what we were so keenly looking for. We were both amazed and delighted to sight the familiar fins of a broadbill swordfish. I changed tackles quickly, while Sid headed the boat towards the fish. He was swimming with a list to port, giving his dorsal fin a slant that was deceiving. Indeed, R. C. and Bob, from some distance, did not identify him as a broadbill. But we knew he was.

All the bait I had was a strip of mackerel and a poor piece at that, but I put it on, and just for fun and curiosity trolled it in front of the swordfish. To my utter astonishment he went down, took the bait, and swam off. I hooked him, and had a couple of electrifying short runs before he threw the hook. It was only then that I realized the thrilling nature of that totally unexpected strike.

Presently Captain Mitchell came along in the little launch. He was tremendously excited. He had seen a large wake in the water behind his bait, then a fish that followed the bait struck it, took it, and went off. The captain hooked the fish, which leaped prodigiously four times, taking over two hundred yards of line, and breaking it. This fish, according to his judgment, must have weighed between two and three hundred pounds. It had a long fin down its back, and broad bright bands round its greenish body, and a long bill. I at once pronounced it to have been a sailfish, and we were jubilant. We fished until afternoon, using the poorest of bait, and then came back to the ship. R. C. was the last in, and he reported seeing a five-hundred-pound black Marlin swordfish that came to his bait and refused it. So the day turned out to be bewildering with its unrealized opportunities.

In the afternoon I watched Romer hook and fight a silver fish near the shore. It leaped high and often. I could see that he was having a hard time of it, but he got the fish, and when he returned was wild with excitement about a new kind of fish and a terrific fighter. We classified the fish as the *gallo*, or rooster-fish. It was indigo blue on the back, silver underneath, very admirably shaped, with long strong body, forked tail, and big head, neither sharp nor blunt. The dorsal fin somewhat resembled the comb of a rooster, at least enough to give it that name. But I thought the name a poor one for so beautiful and wonderful a fish. The natives told us this *gallo* reached a length of five feet, and that information was about the last straw for this bewildering day.

The very next day we captured a large *gallo*, and it happened in this manner. On the way out we trolled off the point and around Black Rock to catch a mackerel for bait. Captain Mitchell was with me, and to illustrate his usual good luck he proceeded to catch what he wanted.

Next I hooked a heavy, powerful fish. It showed to be a shark, and wishing to play a joke on Captain Mitchell I handed him the rod. He began to fight the shark. It very obligingly threw out the spoon, and as the captain was reeling in a large *gallo* took it. What a rush! That fish was lightning for speed and a lion for strength. I felt sure Captain Mitchell would demolish my rod before he could subdue the fish. But at last he got it to the boat, a wonderful specimen of fifty pounds. The colors of blue and rose-silver were exquisitely alive and intense.

On the way up to the White Friars we sighted a broad-bill swordfish and tried to pass him a bait, but did not make a good job of it, and before we could circle him again he went down. A light easterly wind was blowing and there were no fish showing on the surface.

I had seen the White Friars from the deck of the S.S. *Manchuria*, and had thrilled at sight of them, never imagining that I was to fish around them and see a most magnificent spectacle. The White Friars were a group of rocks, large and small, rising sheer out of the sea, and remarkable for their striking shape and white color. At long distance the larger rocks somewhat resembled monks kneeling at prayer, hence the felicitous name.

The closer we got to them the more imposing they grew, until the main rocks, great rock-islands, loomed up in stately grandeur, like marble monuments out of the green sea. The sky was dotted with wheeling wild fowl, and I soon made out that the rocks were literally covered with birds, mostly boobies. We discharged a rifle, and at once a dense black cloud of birds rose, darkening the sun, giving rise to a loud strange roar of flapping wings, and a strong wind that we actually felt pass over us. Thick as a cloud of locusts! A yell was lost in that din. The scream of birds almost drowned the flapping of wings. Soon the roar subsided, as the birds took to sailing, and the lull was as strange as had been the sound. Most of this incalculably large number of wild

ROMER GREY WITH 25-POUND GALLO, OR ROOSTER FISH

PLATE LXXXIII

GALLO, OR ROOSTER FISH. WEIGHT 60 POUNDS. VERY BEAUTIFUL AND GAME FISH, ABUNDANT ALONG THE LOWER COAST OF MEXICO

PLATE LXXXIV

fowl were boobies, the small dark-slate and brown species. I noted many of the white jaegers, with the long
plumed tails, and low down along the rocks, small flocks
of blackbirds that looked like plover. The vast shadows
of wings sailed back to settle down upon the steep white
slopes. This white color, by the way, came from ages of
guano deposited there by the wild fowl, and it was as
deep and rich in hue as if it had been thousands of coats
of white paint.

We made another discovery under the White Friars.
The sea was as full of fish as the air of birds! Monster
gallo and enormous redsnapper, six-foot yellowtail, and
a horde of the other fish—that voracious biter and hard
fighter, the crevalle. We could not troll a spoon ten feet
without hooking a crevalle from ten pounds to thirty.
They got our spoons before the other fish had the slightest
chance. We tried many times, to no avail, and at last,
thoroughly exhausted with fighting crevalle, we gave
up and left the bird-haunted environment of the White
Friars.

A westerly wind had picked up quite a little sea, and
as we started back some one espied a purple fin standing
up out of a green swell. It was slender, sharp, purple in
color, and fully two feet long—the upper lobe of the tail
of an enormous sailfish. I did not need to see the slim
dark body, which came into view, to identify the fish.

We made haste to run in front of him and drag a bait
into as good a position as possible, but though I was sure
he was interested enough to look at it he would not bite.
We tried again, with a small fish for bait, but he was
indifferent to this also.

That was the extent of our adventure for the morning,
except the mere circumstance of having the spray deluge
us whenever we hit a big swell. The sun was very hot
and the cool water most pleasant.

The afternoon we spent on shore, buying parrots, hammocks, quirts, skins, and whatever we could find interesting. I had more opportunity to study the natives and strengthened my conviction that their life was most natural and romantic. Quite violent, too, at times, if the recent fights were common! One man had just killed five men for interfering with the happiness of his wedded existence; and strange to believe, a day before that five men had killed another, for practically the same reason. Señor del Toro told me those men were quick to fight over women. So after all, in that regard, Zihuatanejo was not far behind our civilized communities. But they had not yet acquired habits of appropriating their neighbor's worldly goods.

I watched several boy carpenters at work and marveled at their skill, and especially at the magnificent pieces of mahogany and cedar wood upon which they were engaged. The forests there furnished the finest of timber. Tiles and adobe bricks were baked in crude ovens, but made most effective materials for building the picturesque houses.

The next day, under the guidance of a native named Frederico, we ran up the coast ten miles to a league-long crescent-beached bay, where we went ashore. The white beach extended in a beautiful curve, between the gray-green foliage and the sparkling blue-white sea. Here indeed was a lonely strand, which to walk along would be rapture. While R. C. and Romer and Johnny, with the guide and others, went hunting in a nearby lagoon, I patrolled the beach until the heat drove me to the shade. Waves of heat rose like smoke from the lucent sand. From a shady retreat I watched the wild fowl on the lagoon—the most striking of which was a flock of pink flamingoes.

The hunters returned about noon, laden with ducks,

WHALE ON SURFACE

PLATE LXXXV

WHALE LOB-TAILING

PLATE LXXXVI

snipe, plover, curlew. Romer and Johnny had indulged their hunting ambitions to the full, but not, according to R. C. with any great damage to the wild fowl. It appeared they could not hit the swift-flying birds on the wing, and few other shots presented. Nevertheless, this did not in the least mitigate their immense pleasure.

We boarded the boats and ran out round the headland to the White Friars. I wanted the boys especially to see the birds and try the fishing there. The great white rocks again hummed to the innumerable wings of wild fowl. It was quite impossible to fish, for the birds were actually too thick round the boats. We saw the fish, however, and the sight was perhaps all the more appreciated. I made up my mind to spend a whole day under the white shadows of those sloping monuments, watching, taking pictures, fishing, trying to absorb the atmosphere of a remarkable place.

When we turned shipwards it was to fight the westerly wind and sea; and no longer did we complain of the heat, for the cool spray soon soaked us to the skin. Romer, with dark wet skin and shining eyes, proclaimed to me, "Dad, it was some day!"

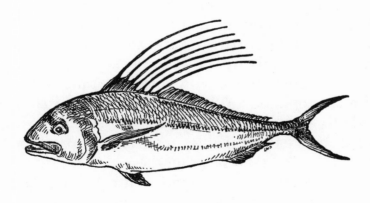

CHAPTER XVI

MORRO ROCKS were some miles up the coast from Zihuatanejo Bay, about as far north as were the White Friars to the south.

But no other similarity existed, unless it might have been that the same felicitousness of name so characteristic of the Spaniards held true. They were rugged, gray, upheaved masses of stone, crowned with grass and low brush, and worn and serrated at the base by the ceaseless wash of the swells that piled and broke upon them.

When we ran by the first rock we were surprised by a loud squawking of parrots; and soon we discerned numbers of macaws flying with the flocks of boobies. They were large green birds, with very long tails of deep blue, and a red topknot. What a clamor they raised! It was decidedly unique and new to fish under flocks of screaming macaws that manifestly resented our presence. Evidently they had their nests on these high rocks.

In the heavy currents and white boiling back-wash from the cliffs we found the *gallo*, or rooster-fish.

My first strike was a smash so swift that I saw only a

flash of green. My tackle was light, of course, but as heavy as we thought proper. Nevertheless, I could not even stop this first fish. He ran round the jagged rocks, and once he was high in a swell above us. Soon he broke off. Then Captain Mitchell had a fine strike from a fish we plainly saw. His broad silver side and his raised black fin, like streamers of ribbons, betrayed him. He hit the spoon, but missed the hook, and he did not come back.

We were using No. 6 Wilson spoons, which we had found the most attractive there for all these inshore fishes. We hooked many redsnapper, crevalle, mackerel, and grouper, which no doubt kept us from hooking more *gallo*. It was strenuous work. A forty-pound redsnapper took time and labor. But we figured out that the fast rooster-fish usually had the first strike in any given place. When he hit the spoon he shook his head fiercely like a bulldog, and usually shook free. We were some time learning this.

The windward side of the second Morro Rock was a turbulent place of seething green and white. A strong current ran in here and the swell crashed to ruin on saw-tooth ledges. As we ran past the outside rock, a yellow treacherous thing, I saw deep blue-green depths and amber shadows. When my shining wavering spoon reached this point I had a solid strike at the instant I saw a black-and-white fish shape. I leaped up to the singing of the reel. My line sped out probably swifter than any time I remembered. At the end of a two-hundred-yard run the fish came out. It would not be correct to say he leaped or jumped: he flew like a silver, black-winged bird. He was a big, powerful, fierce fish, and surely gave me thrills and fears.

Meanwhile Captain Sid got the launch turned, and we chased him full speed, both engines. And then we were just in the nick of time. This fish headed round the corner of the island, beyond the ragged rocks to deep water, where the magnificent swells heaved out of the green and crashed up the ledges. Then as the bottom of the sea seemed to drop a deep roaring gulf slanted from our boat to the green shell-crusted rock, down which white waterfalls were pouring, from tiny streams to heavy torrents.

It was a place I would never have risked myself in a boat containing only one engine. But this little craft had two, working perfectly, and our risk was small.

My rooster-fish ran into that caldron. The heavy swell caught him, lifted and carried him high. All the while he was fighting after the manner of a steelhead trout. I had not the slightest hope of saving him. Suddenly he shot out again, close to us, so that we saw him clearly. He was broad, heavy, white and black; his tail was curved, his eyes seemed large and bold, his open jaws massive. And he shook himself in the air. Right then I fancied I saw in this *gallo* traces of yellowtail, amber-jack, pompano, and especially the permit, which is as great if not as rare as the rooster-fish.

He ran along the whole length of that island, through the thundering surges; and by some miracle of good fortune I led him out into the channel, where I soon subdued him.

When he lay on the floor of the boat I had opportunity to grasp the reality of a new, strange, wonderful fish. But how almost impossible to tell why this was true! The dorsal fin appeared to be a succession of black silk ribbons, broad at the base, tapering to the end of a full foot length. He was massive all over, from huge head to wide tail, the most dazzling silver hue I ever found in any fish. In the sunlight his back was green; in the shadow it was dark. From under the skin changing gleams of pearl seemed to shine.

Always the ocean was yielding some more superlative quality of beauty. Always the beauty! It seemed such a mystery to me. But perhaps nature required beauty as well as other attributes in its scheme of evolution.

When we ran back to the place from which I had lured my rooster-fish, Captain Mitchell hooked another and a larger one. What a rush! Out he flashed twice, and then on the very crest of a mighty swell he limned his beautiful shape against the sky. That was enough for me. I felt unutterably rewarded. But the captain was of another mind, and grimly held to the job of catching this one. And after a tussle of half an hour, now lifted aloft on a huge wave, and anon dropped into the hollow of the sea, with the boom and crash and windy spray all around us, and above the screaming macaws, he finally did it, too.

We tried the other two islands, and were rewarded with several strikes. I hooked one that had too much speed and weight, and with a parting leap out of a patch of white foam he tore loose.

By this time our tackle was practically ruined, the most of which was due to the heavy snappers that we could not avoid. So we called it a day and said good-by to the noisy macaws.

On the fifth day of our sojourn at Zihuatanejo we decided to run far offshore and see if we could locate sailfish or swordfish. I saw one fin that I was positive belonged to a sailfish. Captain Mitchell had two strikes from fish we could not see, but their manner of tugging at the bait, letting go, and coming back to tug again, convinced me these were sailfish also. They were finicky strikers and hard to hook. Captain Mitchell thought he got hold of one of them, but I was inclined to doubt this.

The sun was roasting hot, and seven hours out there burnt us black. I did not suffer from sunburn, but the glare hurt my eyes. When we came in my sight was blurred by dots and hazy patches. What relief the sunset, and later the cool of night! I sat out upon deck listening to the roar of the slow swell around the bay. It was a moving and changing sound, tremendous at times, like the storm wind in the pines, and at others low, deep, melancholy, with a strange note.

Next morning I was rested and eager as ever. The day was cool, fresh, with a faint breeze rippling the water. Before the sun rose the sky was deep blue, and the shadows on the water were reflections of the rosy clouds. The red sun soon changed all that.

We left as early as usual, and trolled along the rocky points for mackerel for bait. I hooked a rooster-fish that ran off with my leader and spoon. We could not catch any mackerel. R. C. had gone out to Black Rock, and was trolling around it.

There was a slow high swell running, very beautiful to see, and the motion was fascinating, but I had learned that such a swell was bad for fishing. My first strike came from a shark that leaped fiercely, turning in the air head forward like the revolution of a steel projectile. He made half a dozen of these wheeling leaps and then threw the hook. Captain Mitchell caught several crevalle, and I caught a yellowtail. R. C. ran by us and hailed us with good news. He had seen a sailfish on the way out to the rock. We wasted a good deal of valuable time trying to catch bait, and at last gave up and headed out to sea.

We had covered a couple of miles when Sid sighted a sailfish on the horizon. He leaped nine times, enough

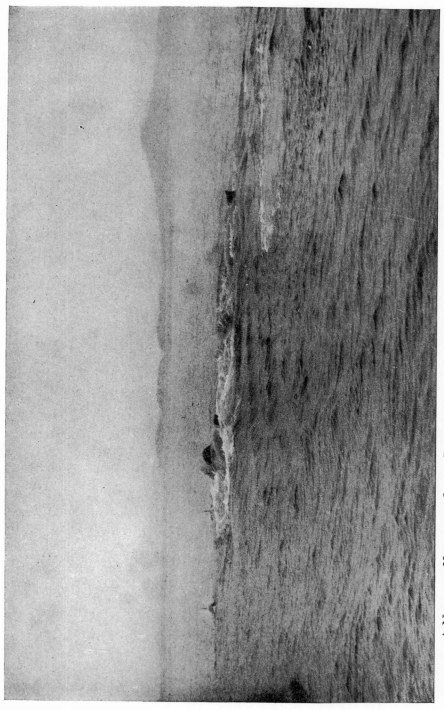

A New and Hazardous Sport, Photographing Sperm Whales on the Surface (Plates lxxxvii to xc)

(The Sperm, or Cachelot, is an inhabitant of warm seas, and perhaps the largest and certainly the most dangerous of all sea creatures. Many whaling vessels have been sunk by sperm whales. His sole food consists of squid and octopus. We had an exciting chase after two sperms, one white and one black. The picture of the white and black tails in the air is considered by the author to be the most remarkable of all his sea experience.)

Plate LXXXVII

PLATE LXXXVIII

PLATE LXXXIX

PLATE XC

for us to see he was big. With both engines at full speed we ran out and were soon somewhere in the vicinity. R. C. followed us closely.

I saw another sailfish way to the eastward, and then, as we began to troll again I espied a big black sail coming out of a glassy patch not far away. We ran for it. Soon it disappeared, and we could only guess where to fish.

Captain Mitchell was trolling with a silver tarporeno, and I was using a strip of yellowtail. We were running at a pretty fast clip, after the method at Long Key. Soon I saw a sailfish leap, a mile away, and not long afterwards one came out within a couple of hundred yards. He leaped twice, curving out sidewise, and showing himself clearly. He was not very long, but pretty broad. I saw his tail several times, and we circled to get in front of him.

I was looking everywhere, except at our baits, when Captain Mitchell said, calmly, "He's got it!" And as I looked he gave a slight jerk. Then followed a crash on the surface. A heavy sailfish came half out as he threw the tarporeno plug high in the air. In my excitement and disappointment I was blunt in telling the captain he should have struck instantly with all his might.

While we ran on we talked about this fish, and the only thing we agreed upon was that it really was a sailfish. Perhaps half an hour later, while we were running parallel with the other boat, we saw R. C. get a strike, and hook a fish. Three times R. C. swept the rod back powerfully. I reeled in my bait in frantic haste and dove for my camera. As I came up with it the sailfish sent the water flying white and leaped out of it. He was long, black, sharp, with enormous spread of sail that flapped like a huge wing. Down he crashed, to pitch aloft again; and that was the beginning of a series of a dozen or more jumps. Out of all I photographed five, and two that I secured were of his spectacular performances. Then he sounded.

In due time R. C. brought him to the boat, and we ran near to get a good view. While they were securing the fish he threshed and lashed the water white. What struck me most, when they drew him aboard, was the extraordinary length. I went on R. C.'s boat to get a better look at this sailfish. He was indeed a wild, strange creature from the deep. His color was a dark amber, very rich and glossy, and dim bars showed along the sides. The sail was black, with spots. His tail was magnificent, very wide and forked, with the lobes tapering to a point. His pectoral fins were truly striking, being two long rapier-like appendages, straight, and black as coal. The extreme delicacy and fineness of all the features about this sailfish were commented upon by all of us. He was certainly a different species from that of the Gulf Stream. His length was nine feet four and a half inches, which was fourteen inches longer than any Atlantic sailfish I had ever seen measured, including the record. The estimated weight was one hundred pounds, very light indeed for his length.

This good fortune fired us anew with zeal; and we went to trolling again. It was my fortune to see a sailfish come shooting back of my bait, his sail half out. I yelled thrillingly, so that all might see. He tapped my bait, took it swift as a flash, sped away. I let him have too much line. Still I was not slow. But he was a wary fish, and as I leaned forward to strike he let go of my bait, and did not come back for it.

For a while my chagrin and disappointment were intense. My first sailfish strike in six days—missed! But after a while the selfish feelings wore away, and the day ended for me with keen sense of pleasure. In all we sighted sixteen sailfish, several of them very large. R. C. assured us he had seen a Marlin swordfish that was a five-hundred-pounder. Chester verified this, and as he was standing on top of the deck, looking down at the swordfish coming for the teaser, his opinion was trustworthy.

That afternoon and evening we spent hours talking and conjecturing, working over tackle, and preparing for the next day. It dawned somewhat cloudy, and the cooler and fresher for that. The sunrise over the mountains was a burst of rose and gold through broken trade-wind clouds. We were off before six-thirty, Captain Mitchell in the small launch with one of the sailors, Romer on R. C.'s boat, and I went alone with Sid and Heisler, one of the mates. We lost no time getting out to Black Rock. A mighty surge was booming and we could not fish as close as usual; nevertheless, we soon caught all the bait we needed. Captain Mitchell went to the westward, while we headed out to sea.

About a mile off Black Rock we espied an Indian canoe with a singular figure in it. Upon near approach we found a young man squatting in one end of the canoe, which was drifting. We had imagined he must be fishing. But he was not doing anything but crouching there in strange dejected posture. He was nude. We hailed him, but all the response we got was the raising of his head. Naturally we thought the Indian was drunk or crazy and we went on our way. It did not appear to be our business to interfere with his peculiar way of being happy.

As we sped out to sea we kept keen watch for leaping sailfish. Not a sign! The morning was perfect, and we were surprised and disappointed not to find the dark ripply water broken by an occasional white splash.

The boobies followed us in flocks, and when we tried

to troll a bait they made it impossible. I jerked my bait away from what seemed a thousand. How they could dive! I amused myself by observing their accuracy. They could dive as true and straight as a rifle bullet. Every time I refrained from jerking the bait they hit it squarely. But if I made a quick jerk, just as they dove, they always hit just back of it, to their evident amaze and anger. Some wise old boobies, after a few ineffectual attempts, sailed aloft ahead of the moving bait, poised to watch it, and they shot down with wings closed. But every time I frustrated this. After a while I grew tired and reeled in my bait until this particular flock of boobies gave up.

About ten o'clock R. C. and Romer had strikes, both of which they missed. We ran nearer to call inquiries, and learned that Romer had missed the same striking sailfish five times, and R. C. once.

"Romer, you've got to be on the job to hook these birds," I called back.

A little later I felt a quick hard rap at my bait. It gave me a thrill, yet I looked sharp, expecting to see a boobie come up from a dive, as I had a thousand times more or less that morning. But no boobie showed. Another rap! I let my line run back. Then my bait was snatched by a voracious sailfish, and my reel whizzed. I performed my part correctly, according to our practice, but I missed him. He took hold of my bait again, and in spite of my speed he let go before I could hook him.

This was all right. I was beginning to appreciate the swiftness, the sagacity, the delicate attack of these Pacific sailfish. It added more zest to the pursuit. After that I stood up most of the time, watching my bait; and as luck would have it, inside of another hour I saw the amber flash of a sailfish as he hit my bait. I let him turn and shoot away before I struck. I felt a solid, irresistible weight. Then the water cracked and the sailfish came out with arrowy swiftness. He looked green-gold-white. The bronze bars shone brightly. He waved an enormous blue sail.

I turned to locate R. C.'s boat, and saw it quite a distance off, coming fast. But I felt they would arrive too late for pictures. My sailfish was out of the water more than in it; only once, however, did he leap high, as had R. C.'s fish. He made twelve jumps, all thrilling and beautiful, then sounded. I settled down to fight him then, and in due time had him exhausted. Towards the end of the battle he stood up on his tail three times, all of which performances Chester photographed. My swordfish tackle was hardly fair to this size fish. When we brought him aboard we all decided he was larger than R. C.'s.

Wind and sea came up, and by noon it was rough. We ran back to the ship. Captain Mitchell had not returned. My sailfish was nine feet five inches long, and weighed one hundred, ten and a half pounds. The spread of his tail was two feet ten inches. The grace and symmetry, the wonderful muscular power, seemed beyond description.

R. C. reported two strikes, and Romer had to confess to the five from one sailfish. About three o'clock Captain Mitchell arrived with a tale of woe. He could not raise a fish with cut bait, so he used tarporenos again. He reported three sailfish strikes; and another from a Marlin, or broadbill swordfish. This fish charged the tarporeno and rushed off with it. Captain Mitchell avowed he struck with all his might. The fish lifted head and shoulders out of the water, showing the red tarporeno stuck in the side of his jaw. He had a massive bronze head and a long bill. He sounded and deep down got rid of the offensive hooks.

We were at a loss what to be sure of. I inclined to the conviction that it was a Marlin. In all my experience, only one broadbill ever charged my bait.

Regarding the sailfish strikes, however, we were all unanimous in our admiration for the remarkable speed and dexterity with which they were made. These Pacific sailfish were very much larger and faster and wiser than their Atlantic brothers. Considering, then, that I had always declared the sailfish of the Gulf Stream to be the finest game fish for light tackle, these of the Pacific began to loom in amazing and bewildering proportions. How could we catch them, if that were possible? How large did they grow? What did they feed on? Where was their range? No angler before R. C. and me had ever wet a line along this lonely coast. It was as wild as the Galapagos. The native Indians went out in canoes hewn from logs, and hugging the protected part of the shore, they speared small surface fish for food. We fished from five to ten miles offshore, and when we turned shipward, after the day's sport was over, we had a magnificent panorama to gaze at all the way in.

When we fished off the Perlas Islands and could see the noble black Andes piercing the clouds, I had been fascinated and deeply thrilled. But I had no idea there could be even a more beautiful sight.

The White Friars shone like creamy snow, kneeling on the blue floor of the ocean. Beyond them began the first low shore range, burned brown by the heat, and this reached to the higher ranges, veiled in smoky haze, that were mere foothills to the grand black Sierra Madres, standing clear and bold above the heat palls. They lifted their peaks to the vast belt of cumulus cloud, the "thunderheads" often seen above the Mojave Desert of California. Vast columns, pillars, temples of gods in the blue sky! They were white and gold, formed with the convolutions of smoke, standing motionless and sublime above the mountains. They were the creations of the intense heat of the sun, and they had lodged against the peaks.

On March 22d, all morning the sea was a dark, glooming, heaving expanse, gray under the soft clouds. It was such delightful weather that almost I did not care whether or not I saw any fish. But I had two strikes, and missed both. I got a jump out of each fish, which Chester photographed, before they threw the hook. The last sailfish was most exasperating.

I saw him coming behind my bait, and leaped to my feet. His sail cut the water, standing above the surface quite distinctly. His color was a bronze-purple. He did not weave behind the bait, after the manner of a cunning Marlin; he just sailed straight at the bait and hit it and took it. As he turned away I clipped on the drag and jerked. Pulled the bait out of his mouth! Releasing the drag, I slacked a little line. He pounced upon the bait again. And again I missed hooking him. This time it was necessary to let back a good deal of line before he snapped the bait once more. Then I gave him considerable line. Nevertheless, when I did strike, the hook held only long enough to fetch him out in a beautiful leap.

That was the extent of my connection with sailfish this memorable day. To R. C. belonged the credit of making it memorable. I had Captain Sid run my boat close to R. C. all the morning; and that was how I happened to be witness to his extraordinary experience.

We saw a sailfish leap near Black Rock, and we ran to troll out baits round the spot. R. C. raised this fish, hooked him, and got a high tumbling leap out of him before they parted.

An hour later, some miles out, we heard a yell that turned us quickly. A long ragged purple fin was shooting behind R. C.'s bait, which was perhaps fifty feet in the rear of the boat. R. C. duplicated my performance of missing three times, and he beat it with a fourth miss. The fifth time, however, with three hundred feet of line out, he finally hung this sailfish solidly. With all that line out there was bound to be a circus. I ran round in my boat, camera in hands, while this game fish leaped thirty-three times. When he was brought to the boat we were all out of breath, especially Chester. We were also beaming, especially Chester, who had photographed every leap.

Not a great while after that Sid's yell made me wheel in time to see another sailfish on R. C.'s line. Its record leap was marvelous—a clean, lofty spring, a turn in the air, with great sail flying, and a dive back. My camera caught the third jump, and my eye began to appreciate the extraordinary length of this fish. We danced round R. C. in our little boat while his sailfish cleared the water some twenty-odd times. After he quit jumping it appeared he took a good deal of hard punishment. We ran close to see the finish. The sailfish came up tail first, apparently entangled in the leader, something that R. C. and I abominate. I saw the broken leader standing out of its mouth. We were to learn presently that the swivel on the leader had cut into the tail, and stuck there, after the leader broke. I not only gasped at R. C.'s announcement of the facts of the case, but also at the wonderful length and slim beauty of this sailfish. He was black with light bars and a purple fin.

But that was not all! In less than thirty minutes R. C. had another big fin behind his bait. He had to tease this fish to bite, and only hooked it after many slackings back of the bait.

CAPE SAN LUCAS, LOWER CALIFORNIA

PLATE XCI

The Beach at Cape San Lucas

PLATE XCII

White spurts of spray! A lean wagging wild bird-like fish-shape in the air! Sid sped up my boat to get back of the sailfish, and I missed a chance at some spectacular leaps. I also lost his location.

Suddenly close to R. C.'s boat there was an enormous splash, and a heavy sailfish, wiggling and waving, clove the air. At the same instant the sailfish on R. C.'s hook leaped splendidly, so close to our boat that Sid had to throw the wheel hard to port. What was our utter amazement then to see, in another leap near R. C.'s boat, that he had *two* sailfish on his line. Sid yelled, "Am I seein' things?" And I yelled back, "You sure are!"

Just what was actually transpiring I could not understand; still I knew it was actual and incomparable.

I lost track of the sailfish on R. C.'s hook, and kept my eye keen for the one tangled up in his line. It leaped repeatedly, so quickly that I was never quite ready. My boat rocked and the excitement was intense. I saw Chester winding the crank of his motion-picture machine, and that afforded me infinite satisfaction. This sailfish quieted down quickly, as far as surface work was concerned, and went to plugging deep. However, in perhaps a quarter of an hour more, R. C. brought it to the boat. Bob got hold of the tangled line, drew the fish close, and grasped its bill. There was some threshing, and flying spray.

The minds of all of us then reverted to the sailfish that had been on R. C.'s hook. It was gone. So was the leader.

We ran close and R. C. said: "Did you ever see the beat of that? Never again can I jolly myself with hard-luck stuff! . . . This blooming sailfish ran past the boat, right at my line, *and began to bite it*. Then the sailfish on my hook made a quick leap, twitching my line over the bill of this one. I saw it happen. He made a lunge, came out, turned over, and twisted up in my line."

I waved to my red-faced and beaming brother. I salaamed to him. I doffed my fishing helmet.

"R. C. you win!" I called. "The plush-lined pajamas are yours. Henceforth I must fish alone."

Remarkable as were all the facts of this capture, it was my opinion that the fact of the sailfish biting at R. C.'s line was the most wonderful. We had seen the same act performed by sailfish in the Gulf Stream. I had not the slightest doubt that it was caused by the instinct of the sailfish to free its mate.

R. C.'s first fish measured nine feet and two inches, and weighed one hundred and nine pounds; the second nine feet ten inches long, and weighed one hundred and thirteen pounds; and the third fish, nine feet three inches, over all, tipped the scales at one hundred and eighteen pounds. If the long slim specimen had been fat instead of lean he would have reached two hundred.

Fishermen, no matter what supreme good fortune befalls them, cannot ever be absolutely satisfied. It is a fundamental weakness of intellect.

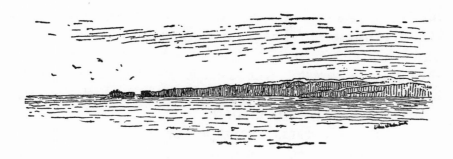

CHAPTER XVII

OUR stay at Zihuatanejo had not reached ten days when we had bought all the parrots and parrakeets the natives could muster.

Romer had nine parrakeets, one of which was so tame it perched on his hand and climbed all over him. Johnny had four. The collection of the Smiths was innumerable. George Takahashi's list included three yellow-head parrots, splendid talkers, in Spanish, of course. The crew also had invested in parrakeets.

My especial prize was a huge macaw, *guacamallo*, the natives called it, for which I had paid twenty pesos. This bird was a beauty to look at, but dangerous to handle. He had a cuning eye and an enormous bill. His color was a glossy green, with tail feathers of blue and maroon. He had a topknot of red. I adopted the name Guacamallo.

At first George chained him, which fact caused trouble. Guacamallo chewed through chain and wire, then ate his way out of cages, chewed the backs off our deck chairs, and made himself generally destructive. There was nothing to do but give him his freedom and let him have the run of the ship.

Guacamallo climbed to the masthead, and out on the radio wire, from which lofty height he sailed clear to shore and alighted in a large cactus, of the kind called pipe-organ cactus. George had to row ashore and climb this thorny tree. The macaw flew into another tree, and when chased out of that he led his pursuer a drill through the forest. But George got him and brought him back. It was difficult to determine which was the angrier, the macaw or George.

Next day Guacamallo jumped or fell overboard, and was drowning when George rescued him. For a couple of days he was a pretty sick bird. After that he recovered, and the narrow escape seemed to have improved his disposition. He lost that evil gleam in his eye. He made no more efforts to escape, allowed himself to be handled, fed, and then caressed, and soon became a pet. He could talk, too, as we discovered, though we could not understand him.

George Takahashi always had a kindly way with pets, and it stood him in good stead here. He soon got on famously with Guacamallo, and in the morning it was a treat to hear him talk to the bird.

"My goodnish, you orful bad bird," said George, one morning, in my hearing. "You make orful mess. You no sleep 'tall where I put you. . . . Here, you drink. . . . Now, Acamalla, behave. You like little boy."

The parrakeets were really a joy. They were small, green-gold birds, with bright dark eyes encircled by a yellow ring. They sang and chattered and talked all day long. Sometimes they would fight, too, especially where there was an odd number.

The wonderful fishing weather continued, one day like that preceding, cool and dark in the morning, with rosy sunrise over an opal sea, gradually brightening to a hot cloudless noon. With the afternoon came the westerly wind and ruffled water. Nineteen straight days of such weather began to spoil us.

Following his remarkable streak of luck R. C. had a day when things went different. To my secret glee! He missed two fine strikes, and then was half asleep when a third sailfish charged his bait. R. C. woke up and got into action, but too late.

Romer fished with me this day. He made endless and enormous preparation, and pestered the patience out of me for new tackle. He had superabundant enthusiasm, until the sun got high and hot and no sailfish appeared. I tried to instill patience into him. This appears to be a virtue that modern boys lack. But finally a big sailfish sailed up behind Romer's bait. I yelled to warn him. The boy did his best, but it was not good enough. Besides, he did not have luck. After the catastrophe was over Romer's active mind began to invent excuses, and before he got through he had me convinced that it was the fault of the fish.

Another hour passed. We scudded over the blue sea, mile after mile, dragging our teasers and baits. The diving boobies quite spoiled Romer's temper and I had trouble in keeping him at the task of fishing. Along about then, however, R. C. had a strike, and that encouraged the boy to carry on.

Another sailfish appeared flashing back of our baits. It rapped Romer's, snatched it and sheered away, swift as a gleam of light. Too quick for Romer! He scored a clean miss. The fish returned, this time taking my bait; and I did no better. What a solace and consolation the boy got out of that!

About noon still another sailfish charged us, getting Romer's bait, and then coming for mine. I was standing, with rod extended, waiting. I saw him hit my bait. I released my reel, letting the line fly off and my bait float back into the greedy jaws. His slender bill came

[157]

out when he took it. As he turned I struck hard several times, and set the hook.

This was a different matter. My tackle was a light one, and I risked it because I wanted sailfish to have all advantage to run and jump. When this one shot out ten feet above the sea, the largest we had hooked, and a most beautiful and superb fish, I was suddenly seized with panic because I had him on such a light rig.

Still I saw with keen eyes his most amazing leaps and surges, his skittering all around on his tail, his nose dives and flying springs. The tension of my line was nothing; it was the hook he felt and wanted to get rid of. Many of his leaps were within a hundred feet of our boat and not far from R. C.'s, where Chester was winding his picture machine. The yelling, the shouts over the cameras, the speeding up of the engines and the throwing out of the clutch, the proximity of the other boat—all these things I was aware of even while intensely set on handling rod and reel.

At that the sailfish got slack line so often that I began to believe he could not shake the hook. Once he stood up three-quarters out of the water, lashing it into foam, and whipping my line so that my rod jerked violently. This in spite of my freely running reel without drag! He was bright silver, with a purple sail as large as a blanket.

Perhaps his contortions did not take up any great number of minutes, but however long this period was it surely left me breathless, weak, and wet with sweat. When he sounded I had another kind of worry. Could I hold him on that light tackle? It developed that I certainly could not. I was afraid to keep on the main drag, and used only the small one, with the additional pressure of my thumb. We followed the fish. If he had chosen to run off I would have lost him. But he came to the surface and swam with the swells, his purple sail waving like a flag. Eventually I wore him out and led him to the boat. It was something of a sight to see that sailfish there in the clear blue water, ten feet out from the boat, swimming along beside us.

"Dad, he made forty-three leaps clear," announced Romer, with his bright positiveness, when we had the sailfish on board. This time it pleased me. "Some fish! Gee! I never saw anything in my life so wonderful. You got him on light tackle, too. I want to try that. He jumped around so much livelier than the others."

My pride in this catch augmented during the succeeding hours. When at last we got my fish on board the ship it appeared that I had reason to be proud, from an angler's point of view.

All the beautiful, delicate, and exquisite features so remarkable in the other sailfish we had taken appeared intensified in this one. He was ten feet one inch in length. He weighed one hundred and thirty-five pounds, and the spread of his tail was three feet.

Through all this fishing R. C. had kept faithfully to his heavy tackle, maintaining that sooner or later he might hook up with some large fish. But he was persuaded to try one day with light tackle. As luck would have it, he hooked a fine specimen of sailfish, which leaped forty times during the hour needed for its subdual. We were thus afforded unexampled opportunity for pictures.

The same day on which this took place I had the very thing happen that R. C. had predicted. It must have been retribution, for all the time I realized what disaster I was courting. Nevertheless, I persisted, taking a chance in the interest of photography.

There are times when the bare statements of fact make

the strongest narrative; and to this end I shall quote a few pages from my note book, exactly as they were written.

March 24.

. . . An hour or more after R. C. captured his sailfish I stood up in the cockpit to ease my cramped legs.

The sea was blue, rippling with slow swell. I heard a solid splash, and looked down to note that some kind of a fish had smashed at the teaser. While I reeled in my bait I called Sid to pull in the teaser. He did so, until it was not more than two feet from the stern, right in the boil of water from the propellers. I saw a flash. Then the teaser disappeared. I thought a sailfish had taken it. I reeled my bait in until the swivel on the leader was up to the tip of my rod. A moving dark color appeared under the bait. Suddenly it was taken by a powerful fish, almost without a splash. I let the line play out, then set the drag, and struck. I came up on a tremendous weight.

The fish broke water with a roar, and I was almost paralyzed by sight of an enormous Marlin swordfish, the largest by far I had ever seen.

It leaped four times, and took line so swiftly I ordered Sid to speed up with both engines. The other boat followed us, and I saw that Chester was beside his camera. We were all excited.

The Marlin shot out like the ricochet of a cannon ball over the water. He hit on his side and skittered with terrific speed across the sea, parallel with our boat and about a hundred feet distant. His back was turned towards us, and I saw his immense girth, fully as large in the middle as a barrel. His length must have exceeded twelve feet. Right there I estimated his weight, too, and was positive it reached six hundred pounds. He went clear round us, in the air all the time, beating the water with his tail. The sound was amazing. When he went down it was in front of our bow and the bag of my line extended far astern.

But we straighted it out, and got behind him to give chase. He started another exhibition of leaping, running his leaps up to thirty. I had more opportunity to study his size. He looked three feet deep at the shoulders. He had a short thick bill. His back was black, which probably identified him as a black Marlin. Broad bars of purple shone from his silver sides. The breadth of his tail made me gasp.

ROMER GREY WITH 66-POUND ROCK BASS, CAUGHT ON LIGHT TACKLE

PLATE XCIII

Romer Grey with 77-pound Rock Bass. This Species Grows to Enormous
Size in the Gulf of California

PLATE XCIV

When he sounded for good and the fight began I realized that I had hooked the most wonderful Marlin I had ever seen on a light tackle—medium rod and fifteen-thread line. It made me sick. It was a terrible catastrophe. There was no hope to defeat such a monster on that rig. The feeling was so strong that it spoiled what otherwise might have been thrilling. But I had no more thrills. I was bitter at myself for such asininity. I complained aloud and to myself.

Nevertheless, I settled down to the hardest battle I ever had on light tackle and I did so because that was playing the game, and I might afford more opportunity for pictures.

I fought incessantly and unreservedly for over four hours, during which the fish took us miles out to sea, and never showed again. I labored under a double strain, that of intense sense of what power to put on the tackle, and that from the muscular exertion I put forth. My arms, and especially my hands, caused me excruciating pain.

Then I found that I could get the double line over the reel. It was staggering. I did it again and again. Thus hope to capture that magnificent fish was born in my breast, and despite all my judgment and common sense it grew all the time. I felt that something might happen. Most of the time we had to chase the fish. But gradually he tired. After four hours and a quarter he stayed close. We saw him often. When I got the double line over the reel and held on for all it would stand we could see him— a huge purple fish-shape, appalling to the gaze. Every time my heart came to my throat.

Then I got the leader up to where Heisler could grasp it. He pulled. Slowly the great Marlin sheered away and upward, coming to the surface, rolling out, his black back, his barred side, and wonderful purple fins bright in the sunlight. I recognized the chance and yelled for Heisler to haul the fish closer. But Sid, in his excitement countermanded my order. Heisler hesitated for the several seconds when the fish rolled there. We had time to get him close and gaff him. But the golden opportunity was lost. The fish sounded.

A dozen times after that I worked desperately, and got the leader to Heisler and then to Sid. But neither could hold the fish. Yet it was plain he was almost exhausted. This quarter of an hour expended my strength. Finally I strained every last ounce of muscle I had for the last time to get the leader up to Heisler's eager hands. Then the double line broke. I saw the gigantic purple fish-shape fade and sink.

Whereupon I fell down in the cockpit and lay there, all in an instant utterly prostrated. When I recovered somewhat and sat up I found I was suffering in many ways—nausea, dizziness, excessive heat and labored breathing, stinging swollen hands, and a terrible oppression in my breast. My arms were numb.

It was a long two hours' run back to the bay. For once the blue sea and the grand mountains had no charms for me. I could not get over the horrible, exasperating, inevitable nature of that catastrophe.

CHAPTER XVIII

IT was fortunate for me that I did not have any strenuous battle closely following the one with the Marlin swordfish. My hands were not in shape for another gruelling contest. But by soaking them frequently in cold salt water I soon hardened the blisters. And as for my sore muscles, good rubbings and plenty of exercise relieved me of the stiffness and pain.

The day succeeding, March 26th, turned out to be our only blank day, up to that date. The westerly wind came up early and by eleven o'clock was blowing hard enough to stir up an uncomfortable sea. We ran in at noon. I had seen one sailfish look at my bait and refuse it. R. C. reported a very large sailfish or a Marlin that did precisely the same thing. Captain Mitchell did not go out. This then was the first day in which we had anything like bad weather—it really was not rough—and that we did not have a strike.

We found an old native on shore, a hunter and fisherman, so his responsible neighbors informed us, who claimed to have measured a sailfish that floated ashore dead. Six meters! That was equivalent to eighteen feet. It seemed incredible, though I have good authority for twenty-five-foot sailfish in the Indian Ocean, off Madagascar Island.

March appeared to be the tail end of the fish season there. R. C. and I wondered what the real season was, if that month was considered poor. We could not, however, get any data on the black Marlin. Probably these great fish were never seen by the natives, for they had only dugout canoes, and could not risk going out to sea. The leaping sailfish, of course, could be seen from shore, especially from the high bluffs.

Next day was perfect. The ocean was like molten heaving glass all morning, and at noon a slight breeze ruffled the water. I caught one sailfish, nine feet three inches, weight one hundred and seven pounds. R. C. had four strikes, missing three, and landing the fourth fish, which was nine feet eight inches long and weighed one hundred and ten pounds. R. C. reported that this sailfish charged his teasers and baits, and he really could not understand how he kept the fish from boarding his boat. I had only the one strike. My sailfish waltzed all over the ocean, in a dazzling performance for the camera.

Captain Mitchell came in with a sailfish, his first, over nine feet, and weighing one hundred and two pounds. He was much elated over this, and at the same time deeply dejected over the loss of a gigantic black Marlin that broke his line. Captain Mitchell said he saw the fish with wonderful black fin above the surface. As he approached it went down, and he lost sight of it. But presently it charged his bait, and came so close that he saw its eyes, large as a saucer. The fish rushed off, taking out three hundred yards of line, and leaping in a way quite beyond description or credence, and broke away. After that he saw two other black Marlin, and seven sailfish. He solemnly assured me that this fish showed itself plainly and was every inch of fourteen feet in length, with weight in proportion. Paige, the boatman, was a Nova Scotia boy who had fished for years on the Grand Banks, and he said it was the largest fish of any kind he ever saw.

About this time these black Marlin began to share most of our waking thoughts, and some of my sleeping ones. Up to this day we had hooked three, and sighted at least four more. They were all exceedingly large fish. It was impossible then for us to ascertain whether or not they were native along that section of the coast, or traveling somewhere, after the habit of all swordfish. Bob King avowed both the Marlin and sailfish were moving north. But I could not see that there was reason for such a statement. I took considerable stock in what the Indian fisherman said.

We spent three days scouring the sea from the White Friars to Morro Rocks for signs of swordfish. During this time the three boats had six or eight sailfish strikes to their credit, and caught three sailfish. One of these days was very still and hot, with absolutely no ripple on the surface of the water from dawn until afternoon. The glare and the heat made long-continued fishing almost unendurable. No sailfish showed this day. There were, however, a considerable number of large sharks on the surface, and the catching of a four-hundred-pound hammerhead was of much advantage to us. He had a dorsal fin almost exactly like that of a broadbill swordfish. It was high, and curved back. The hammerheads of northern waters have a sharp triangular dorsal, broad at the base, and unmistakable to the keen-eyed angler. This was a different species. He had a blue back, and was yellow underneath. He proved to be a stubborn fighter, wearing on angler and tackle. Romer caught a small one, also, and a little later we saw one pass under our boat that had a head four feet broad. What a hideous monster! I let down a bait, and presently, when something took it, I was sure I had connected with this hammerhead. It transpired, however, that I had hooked

[165]

a tiger shark, around two hundred pounds—a vicious swift fish hard to subdue.

Captain Mitchell saw three Marlin that day, one of which took his bait right back of the teaser. He did not hook the fish, so could not judge well of its size. But one of the others was very large. R. C.'s first sight of Marlin swordfish after his teaser came on the following day. Two fish appeared back of the tarporeno, and followed it for over half a mile, very curious, but shy. They would not notice a bait. R. C. said the larger one was thick and long, probably fourteen feet.

For three days a very heavy swell rolled in from the south Pacific. It drove the shore fish we depended on for bait out into deep water, so that we were hard put to it to catch enough. Possibly this surge had something to do with the slackening of the sailfish sport. Still we raised fish every day. In fact there was only one day that we did not get one strike or more. Captain Mitchell had another Marlin follow his teaser for a long distance. Evidently we had not found the best bait for these swordfish. I lost a fine sailfish by getting my line fouled with the teaser, when the fish was running with the hook. What a jump he made! And the hook and bait went flying. A little later I saw six sailfish in as many minutes, one of which loomed up behind my bait, and tantalized me with his splendid bronze and gold. But he waved his purple sail at me and sheered away.

The heavy surge might have spoiled the best of several days' fishing, but I felt more than recompensed by the grand deep rolling music of the swells breaking upon cliffs and strand. I spent hours sitting on deck listening in the cool of evening. Now I was surrounded by a mournful dirge; then a thundering crash broke on the sandy curve before the village. At times there was no sound save a low moaning. But that was always a warning of a coming swell. Boom! It struck the point of rock at the eastern end of the bay, and began its long journey. The ship lifted slowly and gracefully to what seemed a mighty and invisible presence. Thundering and crashing, the vast volume of moving water assailed the cliffs. It passed them and rolled on towards the deep crescent beach of sand, where it rose and fell with a profound long-withdrawing roar. What strength—what sound! The mountains seemed to fling back the deep melancholy echo. It held the mastery of nature in its tremendous action and melody; it was music. The storm winds of the north magnified! It rolled its grand procession round the eastern circle and northern end of the bay, changing, softening, bellowing out like gods of the deep in anger, and lulling to a mournful murmur, full of the wonder of nature and the mystery of life, at last to crash to ruin, and run up the drowned strand. Roll on, remorseless tide! My rapture was inexplicable. And in the watches of the night, when I awakened now and then, I thrilled and quivered to that resonant roar. How grand the Pacific! What a boundless main! And endless shore line! The swell that gladdened my ears and frightened my soul had eight thousand miles of Pacific behind it. I marveled at the thought of all the lonely beaches and wild shores that were beaten by this contending tide. Most of them unseen of human eyes, and so forever!

On our last morning at Zihuatanejo we spent several hours trolling a couple of miles off Morro Rocks. The sea was beautiful, and heaved in colossal swells that lifted us to the skies and anon let us down, down, in the trough. These swells were so long and slow, however, that riding them was a delight. Sometimes R. C.'s boat, with its red umbrella, soared far above me on the crest of a mountain wave, and again it would sink out of my sight, not to reappear for long.

Dolphin played on the surface around us, and swam along beside us, and sported before our bows. Mating turtles in couples scarce took the trouble of paddling out of our way. Boobies and terns swooped over us, with hoarse and plaintive cries. Here and there a sailfish slid out to go high and shine in the sun, then plump back with the sheeted splashes we had come to know so well.

Romer fished with me, and after eight days holding a rod through all the long hot hours without hooking a sailfish he was prone to discontent and the use of wild and whirling words.

We raised four sailfish between seven and eleven o'clock. Each and every one of them was a wary, swift, suspicious fish, and this, in conjunction with an inexplicable stupidity and slowness on my part, was accountable for the fact that the first, second, and third sailfish showed us a clean pair of heels, or fins, so to speak, and got away.

But when the fourth, a big shadowy purple fish, sailed at my bait, and rushed away with it, I got my rod into Romer's hands before the first leap. That, when it came, showed the sailfish to more than average the others. He ran off a lot of line, making us chase him, leaping and tumbling all the time, giving Romer a good deal of trouble, as well as joy. After that he sounded and put up a pretty stiff fight. Romer acquitted himself creditably, and in half an hour had the sailfish up to the boat, within reach of a gaff. But as we did not want to risk pulling the fish in then, we let it run off on a free line, to be rewarded by several slow and final leaps, close to R. C.'s boat. Then the hook came out. Romer was tragic at first, but soon got over that, and was satisfied with the

ROMER GREY FIGHTING TUNA

PLATE XCV

Romer Grey and His 184-pound Allison Tuna

PLATE XCVI

pictures and the fact that we could have gaffed the sailfish.

We let that end our fishing at Zihuatanejo. Not easy indeed was it to quit! Returning to the ship, we turned the boats over to the crew, to be lifted aboard, while we went on shore. We spent the afternoon buying whatever was available from the natives. We had established most friendly relations, and the whole village regretted our departure.

Most of them assembled on the beach to see us launch our canoes through the surf with our precious *ollas*, tame deer, turkeys, souvenirs of various kinds, and last, though not least, an anteater that was tame for its native owner but not for us.

Disaster attended our efforts. A big wave roughly handled the first canoe, breaking *ollas*, soaking us through, and frightening our pets. We essayed again and got beyond the wash of the surf, only to be swamped by an unusually high roller. We were thrown out, but managed to keep the canoe upright. How delightful the cool water! At last we reached the launch and without further catastrophe, though George Takahashi had lost his temper and wrung the necks of the turkeys. The tame deer and the anteater had scratched a good deal of cuticle off Jess, who had volunteered as animal trainer. Eventually we got back on board the *Fisherman*.

It was sunset, and an unusually colorful one, when we passed out of Zihuatanejo Bay, rising to the great, slow, heaving swells that ridged the shimmering water. I gazed back with regret and strange emotion at the line of white beach, and brown thatch-roofed huts, and the green cocoanut palms. Beyond sloped the jungle foothills, rose and gold in the sunset, and above towered the purple range, with peaks lost in pearl-tinted clouds. The primitive village was lost to view behind a jutting point, and soon we were out in the open sea. To the south the White Friars shone dazzlingly bright, in strange contrast to the darkening sea. Westward the Morro Rocks stood up like castles, in black silhouette against the gold of the sunset sky. And the land, from rock-ribbed, surf-beaten shore, lifted by mountain steps, range after range, wild and wooded, to be lost in the clouded sky.

I felt the thrill and pride of the explorer, the discoverer of an enchanted land. How blue and grand gloomed the Pacific, darkening after sunset! What splendid vista of foothill, valley and mountain, and wavering line of dim peaks! Here was a primal untouched world; and Zihuatanejo was practically as wild, lonely, and self-sufficient as when Cortez sailed there in his Spanish galleons to capture slaves.

Right then I knew I would return. And that recalled the giant Marlin swordfish I had so nearly gotten. The long painful fight recurred in memory. I saw his prodigious leaps, his incredible swiftness; and then, when at the end of four and a half hours of battle, he sheered wearily to the surface, his twelve feet of blazing striped purple and silver, his great depth and bulk. Perhaps that poignant memory and the crystallizing sense of loss were necessary to me. Such things always happen! They make for an angler's full experience, for the lessons of defeat so hard to learn, for the appreciation of life in nature, from which comes the soul of man.

CHAPTER XIX

WE sighted leaping sailfish for two hundred miles and more north of Zihuatanejo. Our second morning out we counted nineteen fish, most of them large, and all splendid leapers. One made fifteen jumps, and another tied our record of twenty-one. We were fully eighteen or more miles offshore.

This was tremendously interesting, for we had established with our own eyes, for at least part of the year, a range of six hundred miles for this wonderful game fish. Possibly it travels farther north and south. We had seen a few off the Gulf of Tehuantepec. As we approached the mouth of the Gulf of California the sea became rough, and no fish of any kind showed on the surface. I had no doubt, however, that sailfish ranged as far north as the Gulf.

Somewhere off Cape Corrientes a nor'wester struck us and drove us far out to sea. After the long spell of tranquil tropical water, the hot days and pleasant nights, this gale with its cold wet wind making the vessel toss and pitch was most uncomfortable. We took to warmer clothes and the security of our staterooms.

The seas ran high, great green combers with white crests. They were grand to look at, but decidedly not a joy forever. Not a few of us were seasick. R. C. did not succumb, though he turned the old familiar green shade, and talked pessimistically about the sea fishing.

The menagerie we had on board caused considerable trouble and no end of amusement. The parrots and parrakeets had to be taken below. Guacamallo objected vociferously and escaped up the stairway at every opportunity. The deer, however, appeared to be none the worse for the tossing of the ship.

Our anteater turned out to be some long-tailed, long-nosed species of raccoon. He was as full of mischief as a monkey. When he got loose he had the run of the ship, and there were few places he did not poke his nose. He chased some of the boys out of their staterooms. Only one of the kittens, Checkers, stood its ground when the beast appeared on deck. Checkers was small, but valiant. He arched his back and ruffled his fur, and spat defiance at this newcomer. The raccoon showed no viciousness; evidently he was bent solely on curiosity. But he would snap at the hand that teased him. His favorite sport appeared to be mounting the rail of the ship, and walking along it, oblivious to any peril. He certainly had his sea legs. But one night he disappeared. We expected him to show up sooner or later; however, he did not, and after several days had elapsed we were forced to believe he had fallen overboard. About the same time our little pet squirrel vanished; and as it developed one of the boys had seen the largest kitten, Malty, chasing the squirrel, we decided here was another tragedy of a different kind.

We sighted sailfish over one hundred miles off the mouth of the Gulf of California. I saw three at one time, all large fish, working northwest. This seemed remarkable to me, though I could not give any good reason why sailfish should not be seen far offshore. It might be that they travel north as far as the Gulf, then work out into the Pacific, going somewhere in their mysterious journey.

At daybreak on April 8th we sighted the mountains of Lower California, and soon after that the rugged white outline of Cape San Lucas. We ran into the Gulf to San José del Cabo, reaching it about noon. There was no bay, only an open roadstead, with a long curving white beach backed by green palms, and above and beyond them the stark glaring desert that stretched to the purple ranges. I observed George Takahashi gazing longingly at the land. "Look good to you?" I asked. "Gosh!" he declared, with a grin. "Saved my life!" I had to admit that the sight of land filled me with joy and relief. The last few days, battling a heavy swell and adverse winds, had been very trying. But soon that was all forgotten.

We had to shoot the surf in our skiffs to get ashore, a thrilling and sometimes risky business. But it was fun. The solid sandy beach felt strange and wavy under my feet. Natives in picturesque Mexican garb were unloading boxes of tomatoes from pack-mules, to be transported by canoes to a small freighter lying out in the roadstead. The little town lay back three miles over a dusty green-bordered road, traveled by trains of pack-mules and yelling Mexicans. San José del Cabo had one main street, wide, yellow, deserted, lined on each side by white and brown and pink-walled houses of Spanish design. We found ourselves welcome and that the coming of American travelers had been recognized as advantageous. Our inquiries about fish brought vehement replies, mostly, "*Mucha pescada.*"

The run down the coast from San José del Cabo to San Lucas Bay was a beautiful one, and certainly thrilling. The distance was about sixteen miles, the time late afternoon, and we saw fish enough to satisfy even us. School after school of tuna passed us, and some were feeding on small bait, and others leaping. We saw sailfish, and many whales, and other fish that did not show clearly enough to be recognized. The sunset over the rugged shore line was a reminder of Arizona and the vivid colors of the Painted Desert. It was dusk when we glided into the bay. We could see the lights of other boats, and see a pale wide strip of sandy beach. We dropped anchor in twenty fathoms, quite well out in the bay. The moon came up radiantly, the sea was blanched and beautiful, the roar of surf filled my ears, and the sweet dry fragrance of the desert was a delight.

I was up before sunrise. San Lucas Bay proved to be a wide half-circle sheet of water, with a long silver-banked curve to the west, and the cape running out in bold high hills, bleak and bare, to several monumental rocks that were beaten by the swells. Palms lined the beach. The drab desert of cactus and greasewood sloped up to bald ridges, and these stepped in turn to sharp-peaked ranges. At sunrise the bay was like a shimmering opal. Far inshore were anchored the fleet of the market fishermen from San Diego and San Pedro, California. We counted fifteen. There was a yacht among them.

After breakfast we got our boats overboard, and were soon in readiness to fish. Before going out we took a run over to interview one of the captains of a market boat. He said he recognized the *Fisherman* to be one of the noted Blue Nose schooners from Lunenburg, Nova Scotia. Tuna were running well, he told us, and some of them were big. The fishermen of the live-bait boats catch their fish with hook and line, using live sardines for bait.

So, altogether, it was quite late when we turned the corner of the cape. R. C. and Romer went with Bob, Captain Mitchell and Johnny had the small launch, and I went with Sid and Heisler. We had no bait, and were just on a scouting trip. We had squids, feather jigs, tar-porenos, and spoons. Just off the beautiful sea-carved monument rocks that form the cape we were tremen-dously amazed to see a school of large tuna on the surface.

It would be impossible for me to describe in detail what happened the next few hours. But I had an extraordinary experience, that was paralleled by my companions. My first strike was such a sky-rocket water-throwing plunge that it flabbergasted me. The fish hooked himself, crashed across the surface in white clouds of spray, and shooting off with tremendous velocity took three hundred yards of line in one rush. He never stopped!

Then it seemed I was hooking, fighting, losing, and catching tuna until I was exhausted. During this vio-lent, hazy wild period I had occasional accidental glimpses of my comrades in the other boats doing the same thing. It was like a dream. Tuna everywhere! One of the market boats shared our luck and labors. Every time I chanced to glance at this boat I saw two fishermen hauling on hand lines, with a fish on each.

I hooked and lost three very large tuna. Besides these I lost a number of others, none under a hundred pounds. Leaders, swivels, tarporenos, broke for me. I had a big tuna strip a tarporeno of hooks. My twenty-four-thread line was broken twice. But I caught eight tuna, the largest being two hundred and eighteen, one hundred and eighty, and one hundred and fifty pounds, respectively. I broke the rod-socket in my chair, and finally the chair itself. So after that I ran out to see how it fared with my comrades. I found Chester fighting a fish out of R. C.'s boat, and farther out Captain Mitchell and Johnny were both fighting a tuna at the same time. It was bewildering, exhilarating, and funny. When at last we all got back to the ship we were an excited and tired crowd of anglers. Romer had caught a tuna of one hundred and forty-three pounds and he was overjoyed. The others accounted for seven more. R. C. reported some tremendous strikes and lost fish. Captain Mitchell and Johnny had but one. The captain had his heavy tackle smashed twice. We had been unprepared.

The consensus of opinion was that the tarporeno was a most attractive lure, but a signal failure. It did not hook more than one fish out of five strikes, and did not hold that many when fish were hooked. We had taken the precaution to put on larger and stronger hooks. But the brass eyes opened and the rivets pulled out. The feather jig with large hook had the better record.

These fish were of the long-finned species, closely allied to the Allison tuna. In my opinion they were not the yellow-fin we have in Catalina waters in August and September. Also they differ somewhat from the yellow-fin we caught at the Galapagos Islands. Their flesh was remarkably solid and heavy, and that was why, as the scales proved, we guessed their weight so incorrectly. Brilliantly colored, blue, gold, bronze, silver, mother-of-pearl, and so perfectly shaped to combine speed and strength, they were exceedingly beautiful fish.

It was fortunate that we had the tuna fishermen there to take these fish gladly off our hands. Otherwise we could not have felt well over the wonderful day, let alone plan to catch more. Tuna steak for supper received hearty commendation from all on board the *Fisherman*.

The question of tackle for these hard-striking, long-enduring tuna assumed all importance that evening. Romer and Johnny made theirs to suit themselves. Bob worked on a wonderful but doubtful improvement of the tarporeno, and Sid made new leaders with different kinds of lures. One was a feather jig, fashioned after those

ZANE GREY FIGHTING TUNA

PLATE XCVII

WEIGHING LARGE TUNA

PLATE XCVIII

used by the market fishermen, only with a large hook to suit my idea. It was a very ingenious device, this feather jig, as developed by the professional fisherman; and it consisted of a small metal case, about the shape of a cartridge and the size of a man's finger, with a hole running through, and a screw cap fitting into the large flat end. The leader was strung through with the hook on the end, then the feathers were stuck in at the large opening, arranged deftly, and the cap screwed down. The boys rigged tarporenos in the weirdest of fashions, armed with two big sharp hooks, through the eyes of which the leader went. I preferred the smaller tarporeno with a single large hook that separated from the wood, once the fish was hooked.

Next morning we were up bright and early, finding, to our dismay, a strong westerly wind blowing, and an overcast sky. Nevertheless, we ran out beyond the cape. A rather choppy sea promised discomfort if not poor fishing. Romer was with me, keen to use my tackle. Before we had gone a quarter of a mile he had a smashing strike. The tuna ran off all the line and broke it, or it was cut by another fish. Such things often happened and could not be avoided. Romer lost the leader he had labored hours to perfect. He was disconsolate. Youthful fishermen are prone to bewail even the littlest disasters. "Aw! that'll spoil my day!" he wailed. But I kept him on the rod, and soon he had a strike that dwarfed the first. The water shot up in a boiling white splash. This tuna ran three hundred yards. When he stopped and Romer got most of the line back, we figured that he had hooked a heavy tuna. So it turned out. Romer had the longest hardest fight of his fishing experience, already quite extensive. He gave a fine exhibition for a boy. The whirling of the seat bothered him greatly, and I had to hold the seat firmly and turn it as occasion demanded, so that he could put his strength into the rod.

Eventually he whipped this tuna, the size of which, as it came up in the clear water, brought a loud hurrah from the boy.

I took the rod then, and in the succeeding hour had three strikes, without hooking one fish. The wind freshened and it began to be more labor than sport to stick in the boat. I had observed from time to time that Captain Mitchell and Johnny were tied up with tuna. Once when we ran close we were in time to see Captain Mitchell break a fine hickory rod I had presented to him. R. C. had George Takahashi with him, and I could not see what was happening to them. We ran in before noon. There were no tuna on the surface, and the day did not look fishy.

Yet when we tallied up it turned out to be remarkable fishing, even if the weather was bad. R. C. had two fish, not very large; and he reported a tremendous strike for George. Captain Mitchell and Johnny caught eight tuna, the largest, credited to the captain, being one hundred and seventy-one pounds. The others averaged around one hundred and thirty.

Romer's tuna was a splendid specimen weighing one hundred and eighty-four pounds, and he was mighty proud of his achievement. "I don't want to tackle another for a few days," he said.

Takahashi's comment on the day was characteristic. "Me seasick first thing. Felt orful bad. But when big tuna smash at my hook I see him and forget all about seasick!"

We scraped acquaintance with several captains of the fishing boats, and made it a point to run over to see them occasionally, after the day's fishing. There were three purse-net boats, half a dozen large live-bait boats, and several small ones, besides the cannery tender, and a large schooner that was used for cold-storage purposes. The fishermen returned at evening to sell their catch of tuna at forty dollars per ton. These fish were frozen in the cold storage plant on the schooner, and presently transferred to one of the cannery tenders, which took them to San Diego or San Francisco. Among the fishermen were some Japs and Austrians, but most of them were Americans.

Captain Heston, of the schooner, had been following these tuna for eight years. In answer to my queries he made some interesting disclosures.

"I have not noticed any diminution in the number of yellow-fin tuna. There are as many now as when I first started in this business. And that means millions. Some years there are not so many, other years are good. This year they are thick. Tuna spawn on the bottom, and one tuna will have a thousand eggs where a salmon has one. They multiply tremendously. Probably that fact will save the tuna from extinction.

"We prefer the small ones, from forty to sixty pounds. There are a good many brought in from two hundred to two hundred and fifty. Occasionally some over three hundred. The larger ones are hard to catch, and the live-bait fishermen try to dodge them. I saw one harpooned that was the largest in my experience. He was nearly ten feet long, and might have weighed seven hundred pounds. He got away with the harpoon.

"This year we have been with the tuna all the time. We followed the schools up the coast as far as Cedros Island which is about as far as the main school runs. We stayed there with them, and then came back here with them. Two months ago as we came south into the Gulf with the schools we passed other schools working north. The ocean was alive with tuna."

CHAPTER XX

ROMER and Johnny were given instructions to take the small launch and troll along the rocky west shore, and the sandy northern shore in search of white sea bass and yellowtail. They were full of zest and importance, and made another raid on my tackle trunks. I took Captain Mitchell with me.

The sunrise was rosy and gold, shining on an opal sea as smooth as glass. Along the beach the market fishermen were hauling their nets for bait. Range and desert shone rosy in the morning light. A low wash of surf broke the sweet silence. The freshness of spring, the warmth of summer filled the air.

We were out on the sea before seven o'clock, ahead of most of the market boats. Schools of bait, dark patches of water that denoted tuna swimming deep under the surface, black fins of sharks, white and black rays, leaping high to flip over and over, and now and then a splash, greeted our eager eyes whichever way we looked.

Before we had a tuna strike we ran into a school of young porpoises. They were jumping, rolling, and slapping the water with their flat tails. Occasionally one would shoot high into the air, turn over and go down. We followed them for a couple of miles, taking pictures, and enjoying the life, color, and movement. Then Captain Mitchell had a strike, which put an end to my photography, and to his leisure for a while.

After catching three small tuna in this locality we ran east and several miles out. There were no signs of fish on the surface. R. C. had worked off to the eastward of us, and the market boats slowly grew dim in the distance. Presently I hooked a tuna that took more than three-quarters of an hour in landing. He weighed one hundred and seventy-four pounds. Then Captain Mitchell had his turn.

This tuna was a fighter, and seemingly grew stronger as the battle progressed. Captain Mitchell's rod got jammed in the rod-socket, and could not be removed, and the reel-seat became loose. This almost amounted to disaster, as the captain had great difficulty in subduing the fish. It took nearly two hours. The tuna was one of those built on long lines. He weighed one hundred and eighty-five pounds, and was Captain Mitchell's largest to date.

Soon after letting out my line I saw a flash of silver and a swirl behind my feather jig. A cracking smash, making a huge patch of white water, was followed by a terrific lunge on my line. It jerked me out of my seat. Despite the grip I had on my rod I almost lost it.

The tuna shot along the surface, between two green furrows, showing a broad back, and as he went he surely gathered headway. I yelled for Sid to chase him. That became the most spectacular surface run I ever saw. It was incredibly swift. My reel shrieked as the line shot off. A remarkable feature also was the length of line out of water. Fully one hundred yards! Beyond that stretched two hundred yards more, whipping the water white, as the tuna dragged it in a curve over the surface. He had four hundred yards out, and for a considerable number of moments before we began to gain. We chased him some distance before he sounded.

Then I settled down to a grueling contest. The depth

at which the tuna worked added much to my difficulties. For two hours I labored hard and persistently before I made any obvious impressions on him. He was heavy and tireless. No doubt about the punishment he inflicted upon me. But at last I got him to the surface, where the size elicited yells from all of us. He turned head down and dove. As he gathered momentum my reel began to shower me with spray. In a few seconds he took off half of my line. That with the drag on! When I had to release the drag I bade him good-bye. After one thousand feet he slowed up. But he went on down until he had reached a depth of thirteen hundred feet. When he stopped I endeavored to lift him. Not an inch! Harder I pulled. Presently the dead weight slightly moved and I recovered a fraction of line. I had to lift with all my strength. But that was not very great now, as I had overworked. Excitement and hope revived me, and I strained every muscle. The time came when I could lift him and gain several feet of line; and of course the farther up I got him the less the tremendous strain. In what seemed an age I lifted him to the surface, a blazing blue and yellow monster. It took both boatmen and Captain Mitchell to haul this tuna into the launch. The magnificent flaming colors, blue, gold, silver, opal, pink, bronze, changed marvelously every second, and were most strikingly beautiful as he quivered and died. This tuna measured nearly seven feet in length and over four in girth. He weighed three hundred and eighteen pounds.

Late that afternoon R. C. returned, with telltale white circles under his eyes. I saw them even before I saw the boat—full of tuna. He had nine, two of which were caught by Chester. The largest weighed one hundred and ninety, one hundred eighty-three, one hundred seventy-nine, one hundred seventy-five; and the rest were around one hundred pounds.

"Some day!" said R. C. when he got aboard, and he gave that queer little laugh. "We found a school of big fish and stuck with them all day. I licked one that was big—around two hundred and fifty—and got him up to the boat, only to have the hook pull out. But say, it was with one of Chester's fish that we had a wonderful experience. Right after the strike the tuna went down deep. Suddenly he stopped. The rod ceased to nod. Chester looked queer and said: 'He feels different.' I thought one of the great leopard sharks had got the tuna. I got Chester to let me take the rod, and when I did so I felt the strangest weight and sensation I ever had from the end of a line. Something was dragging, working, mauling the tuna, causing a peculiar rotary motion. Bob came back and took hold of the line, but he couldn't budge it. 'Somethin' mighty big an' heavy. Must be a shark. But then it doesn't feel like one.' Bob was persistent and struggled to lift our fish and its captor. It was terrible labor. After a half hour he got perhaps a hundred feet of line. Then, just when we anticipated seeing it any minute, the tremendous live weight let go. He hauled up a tuna, dead as a door nail, and all scarred and circled by queer marks, abrasions on the skin. These had been made by the suckers of an octopus. There's absolutely no doubt of it. Come and look at the tuna."

I examined the fish with intense interest, and if the white ridges and welts on its body had not been made by an octopus I have not the slightest idea what could have caused them. My conviction was that they had indeed been made by the octopus, the monster devil-fish of the Pacific.

Romer, too, had a tale to relate, one of wild whirling words. He had hooked several large white sea bass in the bay, and Johnny had enjoyed a losing fight with a fifty-pound yellowtail. Then Romer had hooked a small fish which was immediately savagely attacked by an enormous rock bass. In its efforts to devour the small fish it got Romer's hook. A two-hour battle on three-six tackle ensued. "I didn't hope to catch that fish," said Romer, "but it was a larger rock bass than I ever dreamed of. So I worked till my hands and fingers were dead. We followed him all along that beach, into coves and close to the rocks. Finally I got him up—on that light rod and line! Johnny gaffed him. Sixty-five-pound rock bass!"

Before I saw the fish I doubted the classification of it, but upon examination it turned out to be indeed a rock bass, the largest by far that we ever heard of. Romer was prouder over this capture than that of his big tuna.

He had more to tell. They had happened upon a gigantic ray, one of the species that Captain Heston said frequented San Lucas Bay. It was fully twenty-five feet across its back. Paid no attention to the boat!

"We were afraid of the thing," averred Romer, "but when Johnny yellew, 'Soak the big gaff into him!' like a fool I did! He nearly swamped the boat. Made right for us! Threw great spurts of water up! Then he straightened out the big gaff and got away. . . . Say, it was the most wonderful day I ever had. Some place this Cape San Lucas! Isn't it great to get a lot of bites from big fish, and see strange things?"

Romer had voiced the truth. There was something wonderfully thrilling for an angler in this beautiful bay, with its wild shore line, and the incredible number and size of the game fish. It was heart-satisfying.

What transpired on our next tuna venture, I shall always remember, for the day was one of unmatched excitement, with a climax of excruciating pain.

Captain Mitchell was again my companion. The day was perfect, the sea a glancing heaving blue. We ran out a couple of miles to where the market boats were work-

TWO-HUNDRED-AND-FIFTY-POUND ALLISON TUNA

PLATE XCIX

ZANE GREY AND 318-POUND ALLISON TUNA, CAUGHT AT CAPE SAN LUCAS

PLATE C

ing. Rushing strikes were soon in order. The captain and I had a double-header. He lost his fish. I caught mine. We went on. A purse-seine boat was making a haul. We stopped to watch awhile. The great net was full of tuna—so full the dozen or more men could scarcely move it. "Forty tons!" the captain yelled.

I put out a tarporeno teaser, and sat with my camera ready, hoping to snap a tuna strike at close range. Captain Mitchell wound his lure close to the tarporeno. Suddenly the green water exploded in a white fountain-burst. I snapped that splash. Then Captain Mitchell fought the tuna he had hooked for over an hour, broke his rod square off, yet saved the fish. We had several more strikes, catching two tuna; then both our white feather jigs were demolished. Captain resorted to a piece of canvas, while I used the last jig I had.

It was fun to watch the tarporeno. That wooden plug surely had a hard time. A school of small tuna attacked it and afforded us much amusement. Then a big fish snapped the heavy cord and pitched the tarporeno fifteen feet into the air. As it came down another tuna hit it. Then Captain Mitchell connected with another battle. This time he only broke a leader.

Sid called out that he saw another school of tuna. We ran into it. I saw the dark leathery fin of a basking shark stick up out of the water. It was immense. But before we could get near enough for a picture it sank. Next we had another double-header. R. C.'s boat came along, and Chester had fun taking motion-pictures of the captain and I changing seats, passing one rod under the other's line, and back again, all while both tuna were running hard. Marvelous to relate, we saved both fish, in something like an hour's battle.

R. C. was having a bad day. We espied him get strikes, hook, fight, and lose fish. We saw him catch several. On another tuna I lost my last feather jig, but I landed the fish. Then we drifted on the sea and ate our lunch. The market boats were all around us, hand-lining tuna. The men were dexterous, strong, and tireless, but we observed that the big tuna got away.

When we started in again I arranged an extra rod, with a long leader and a baited hook. This was for quick use in case we raised a sailfish or swordfish. Not long afterward we did raise one—a Marlin. He glided up on Captain Mitchell's canvas lure, and while I yelled orders and got rid of my rod to snatch up the other, the Marlin almost reached the teaser. He darted at it just as Heisler jerked on the cord. How the wide purple pectoral fins stood out!

He dropped back as I let out my bait. Then he came for it, but not on the rush. When I pulled it back he sailed ahead and took it. The reel whizzed. I had not lately used the Vom Hofe reel, and could not set the drag quickly enough. The swordfish leaped, and threw the hook and bait far from him. I saw him clearly, and estimated him about four hundred pounds. What a crash when he fell back into the water!

Following that incident I had strenuous exercise on a husky tuna, while Captain Mitchell mended tackle. Then followed a couple of hours of violence which could not be adequately recorded in memory. I finally was reduced to a tarporeno. This I had rigged on a double leader with a single large hook.

Captain Mitchell got patched up again, with a canvas bait out—the same kind on which he had seven strikes —and we were speeding along with a little breathing space. Not for long! Smash! The water cracked, boiled, spurted at the captain's bait, and—bang—his rod was jerked down on the gunwale. At the same instant a curling roaring hole split in the water, and a large tuna appeared, moving like a flash, tail toward us. He hit my tarporeno with tremendous force. The surface run that followed was magnificent, indescribable, and unbelievable. When he sounded I had my hands full. An hour's labor brought the double line over my reel, and shutting down on it I held fast. This tuna proved to be a weaver. He went round and round at the stern of the boat. I thought he would tire, but he did not. However, I did! He would pass the stern, sail up on the surface, flip his tail, dive, and turn on his side, then clear over, and come up past the stern again. I saw that one strand of my leader was broken. So I dared not trust either of the boatmen to pull on it. I wound my line up so that the leader was out of the water. And then I held him. There was no need to let him run off with more line. I would only have had to pump him back. When he sailed upward to the surface the strain on my back and hands was released, but when he dove he lifted me right out of the seat. He kept this up. All the time I was waiting for him to tire. It grew to be almost unbearable, yet somehow I held on. I had hooked many weavers, but this fellow broke all records. Finally I had to hold the double line with both hands. The rod wagged up and down, up and down. An ordinary tackle would not have stood that strain for a moment. Gradually he circled slower, and that gave me the strength to hold on. The boatmen and Captain Mitchell, seeing what pain I was suffering, made all kinds of suggestions. But I heeded none.

For over two and a half hours that tuna performed this peculiar weaving circle, all the time in plain sight. He was long, wide, thick, a blazing silver at one time, at another yellow and green. He made the circle several times a minute, until towards the last. When he weakened perceptibly, slowed his wide swerve, swam more on his side, I knew if the tackle held that I would get him. I noted then how he was coming closer in to the boat, and I called Sid to come back beside me with the long gaff. This he did, and presently the tuna came within reach. When Sid gaffed him there was a flood of water over us. He gave both boatmen a tussle to hold him.

It was five o'clock. I had fought that tuna four hours. My hands and arms were dead and I could not stand up straight. There was no room in the boat for the tuna, for all available space was full of fish. We towed him back to the ship, where our arrival was a thing of moment.

We had eleven tuna, seven credited to my rod, and four to Captain Mitchell's. His fish weighed respectively two hundred and two, one hundred seventy-five, one hundred sixty, one hundred forty-five pounds.

My large tuna weighed two hundred and fifteen pounds, and the others were one hundred ninety-eight, one hundred eighty-five, one hundred seventy-nine, one hundred seventy-five, one hundred seventy-one, and one hundred and thirty-five.

This catch so far exceeded anything I ever did before that I seemed unable to realize it. I was all of nine hours on the rod, and that last battle was something to make me infinitely respect these Allison tuna.

That day one of the live-bait boats brought in a Marlin swordfish, and we went over to see it.

The fish was a magnificent specimen, twelve feet long, four feet ten inches in girth, and weighed over six hundred pounds. It had a short bill, a small head, and a very heavy body, carrying its weight clear to the tail. The color was dark, so dark that the stripes were indistinct. The fins appeared to be less pronounced than in the Marlin caught at Catalina, but the tail was much wider. I never before saw such a noble fish, out of the water. After careful consideration I saw the close rela-

GIANT BLACK MARLIN SWORDFISH, 690 POUNDS, CAUGHT BY MARKET
FISHERMEN AT CAPE SAN LUCAS

PLATE CI

One-hundred-and-eighty-pound Striped Marlin Swordfish, Caught by R. C. Grey at Cape San Lucas

PLATE CII

tion of the swordfish to the one I had such a losing fight with at Zihuatanejo. With this one for comparison I was convinced I had lost a still larger fish. This was the black Marlin.

The market fishermen saw seven others of this species, five in one lot. I was inclined to think, however, that they could not tell the difference between the two species. The Catalina Marlin were not common in these waters, and I could not learn where they came from. My opinion was that they worked up from the south. None of this species had ever before been taken. It was amazing as well as dismaying, to learn that this incomparable Marlin swordfish had been caught on a hand line, on a hook baited with a white rag. The market fisherman was trolling for tuna at the time.

Sight of this fish gave us the swordfish fever, so we devoted next day to hunting Marlin. I did not have any luck. Captain Mitchell had one strike. R. C., however, raised two Marlin, one of which he caught. It was nine feet and weighed one hundred and seventy pounds, and was not a black Marlin. After capture its colors were exceedingly vivid and changing. The pectoral fins were purple, the dorsal and tail lavender, the body a wonderful shade of silver, and the stripes were pale blue. The other fish that R. C. raised was a black Marlin, of huge dimensions. It came up attracted by the tarporeno teaser, and followed the boat, refusing to look at a bait. Bob King said: "He was just curious aboot that fool tarporeno. He knew there wasn't such a crazy fish in the sea, but he just wanted a look at it."

This incident brought up again the question of the utility of tarporenos. We had discarded them as baits, retaining them only as teasers. The singular gyrating motion of a tarporeno in the water will attract the attention of fish. That was about all it could be guaranteed to do. And it began to dawn upon us that few of the fish brought up by this lure would look at a bait. They were curious about the wiggling, sheering, diving, colored plug. So curious that a real bait did not interest them! This made the tarporeno even an unsatisfactory teaser.

I had another chat with Captain Heston. His years of experience along the Mexican coast made him an exceedingly interesting fisherman to listen to. He certainly cleared up the albacore question, that had perplexed Avalon boatmen and anglers for years.

Albacore used to run north as far as Santa Cruz. The fishing for them around Catalina made a lucrative business for professional fishermen and boatmen alike. But of late years the albacore had grown scarcer and scarcer, thinning down to a few schools, and last summer, 1924, very few reached Catalina waters. "All gone! Fished out!" declared the interested persons.

Captain Heston informed me that during the same season along the Mexican coast below San Diego, there was a hundred square miles of albacore, an endless, boundless school beyond all computation. For a month the hundreds of boats filled to capacity every day. The price of fish was cut in half, then to less. The canneries were flooded. This brought a strike on the part of the market fishermen, which ended the fishing for the season.

The point Captain Heston emphasized was that there were more albacore than ever. No one could tell where. They just changed their run. They grew wise, and did not go so far north. Thus they would be forced farther and farther south.

The blue-fin tuna learned their lesson. Once they could be caught—or hooked—with ridiculous ease from a rowboat on any kind of a bait. As the years went by they began to learn, until the time came when a kite was necessary to drag a bait over a school. Last summer boats dared not go anywhere near a surfacing school of tuna. Presently they will not be fooled even by a kite.

The yellow-fins are apparently stupid pigs. They school in myriads and are ravenously hungry. Boats, men, baits, jigs, gaffs have no significance for them yet. Nature has not yet warned them.

I saw one of the live-bait market boats in action. A school of yellow-fins had been drawn round the stern. Three fishermen leaned over with short thick poles, rigged with a two-foot leader and small Japanese hook, on which wiggled a live sardine. These baits were dropped, dangled on the surface. Scarcely under the water! Another man stood behind throwing out live sardines from a live-bait tank. Another brawny fisherman stood with the three, and he was armed with a short gaff and a baseball bat. Boils and swirls on the surface of the water, right under the stern, attested to the active presence of tuna.

Then one of the fishermen lurched, struggled, heaved on his thick pole. Out splashed a seventy-pound tuna. He seemed to jerk it right at him, and caught it under his arm. He wrenched out the hook, dropped the tuna to the deck, where it was dispatched by the brawny man with a baseball bat. R. C. and I could not but comment on such use for the famous Louisville sluggers—the baseball bats we once knew how to use so well.

They caught half a dozen small tuna in short order, working like machines. Then that order was suddenly changed. One of the fishermen hooked a big tuna. Surge and roar! He heaved mightily—got the shining head out, then the wide back. The brawny helper leaned over with his hook and struck it deep into the fish. White water obscured both men and stern of boat. The splashing subsided, and then we saw four fishermen strenuously

[191]

dragging a two-hundred-pound tuna up over the stern. It had not taken five seconds to hook him, start him up, gaff him and drag him aboard. The fish had no chance to get into action.

Right after that smaller ones were caught. Next a larger one gave the four men a short, terrible struggle. What thumping splashes! He nearly dragged all of them into the sea. They had two gaffs in him, besides the hook. But he was too much for all the men. He broke away, taking rod and gaffs with him.

I was thrilled at this battle, interested to see that particular kind of commercial fishing. I will say that it is a fair strenuous game. Hook and line! They earn every fish they catch. It takes hardy men to stand such work.

But what struck me most was the stupidity of the yellow-fins. They had not yet learned the deadly enmity of man. Nature in time will teach them, and that kind of fishing will pass.

LEAPING DOLPHIN AND PORPOISES (Plates ciii to cx)
(These are different species, as explained in text. They play on the surface for hours.)

PLATE CIII

Plate CIV

Plate CV

PLATE CVI

PLATE CVII

PLATE CVIII

PLATE CIX

PLATE CX

CHAPTER XXI

THE style of fishing has more to do with the thrilling effectiveness of a strike than any other thing.

Trolling from a fast-moving launch has always been the most exciting and fascinating method in angling for heavy game fish. The reason is because the strike is electrifying and strenuous. The bait or lure is speeding through the water. The fish chases it. He hits it. Then the angler sees the surface commotion and gets the solid shock when fish and hook meet.

The strike from a tarpon, hitting a fast bait, is strong enough to jar an angler. That of a sailfish is different. It is delicate and light, comparatively. Marlin swordfish at Avalon usually slip up easily, rap the bait, take it, and flash away. But sometimes a Marlin will rush a bait and make a great splash. The black Marlin evidently rely less on stunning their prey with their bills than the smaller species. They have shorter bills, although all the rest of their bodies are larger. These black Marlin are as quick as lightning, and make a rushing strike that is a shock both to mind and body. It is a beautiful swirling white strike. Bob King was felicitous when he said, "They shore put it in high!"

The giant Nova Scotia tuna, if he struck a trolling bait, would demolish the tackle and jerk the angler overboard. I have no idea what a splash he would make, but it would be tremendous. Blue-fin tuna at Catalina, hitting a bait attached to a kite, make a thrilling strike. A bulge appears behind the skipping bait, then the tuna dives. Smash! He makes a round cracking circle of foamy water. The blue-fin hitting a trolled bait—as was the method before kite-flying—makes the same kind of a strike, only magnified every way, and of course the angler gets the full benefit of that powerful smash.

The Allison tuna, to my thinking, strike swifter and harder at a moving bait than any of the above mentioned fish, barring what the Nova Scotia tuna might do. They make a hole in the sea, and a roaring splash, that would do justice to the plunge of a horse from a high cliff. I never before experienced anything so terrific as the strike of one of the large Allisons. We trolled from a fast-moving launch, at greater speed, in fact, than even in sail-fishing. We set our drags as tight as we dared. Of course the instant the tuna hit and hooked himself we knocked off the drag. If we could! Tuna of three and four hundred pounds, shooting like a bullet through the water, suddenly coming up solid on a line, gave us the angling shock of our lives. It was bewildering, stunning. Then their habit of thumping around, making the water fly, and running off on the surface with amazing velocity added so much more to their strike. Allison and yellow-fin tuna are rated below the blue-fins at Catalina. Whatever they may be there, in the Gulf of California and along the Mexican coast they are a swifter, stronger fish. They weigh more. We underestimated every one from ten to forty pounds.

As to tackle, common sense would dictate the use of the best and heaviest that could be bought. Even then there will be broken leaders, lines, rods. During our first week at Cape San Lucas two anglers from Des Moines were there on their yacht. They had a lot of light tackle up to twenty-four-thread lines. And included were one hundred of the feather jigs. When they quit, after a week's fishing, they had six jigs left, and no lines. We saw them get cleaned out time and again.

One of these anglers frankly and disgustedly admitted to R. C. that it was ridiculous to try to stop these tuna on light lines, leaders, swivels, etc. Experience is the best teacher. These men did not know, and they had been misinformed. It is a pretty safe bet that they will never forget their experience, and never repeat it.

Captain Mitchell brought out the point of the matter very simply. "No salmon fishermen would go after forty-pound salmon with a four-ounce rod and a silk thread. Tackle for heavy, strong fish should be heavy and strong. Common sense ought to tell an angler what to use. It would, too, in almost all cases, where a man had not been prejudiced or ignorant. What is the sense in breaking or losing a new line on every fish, in the hope of hooking one he could hold? Consider the expense, not to speak of the disappointment. There is much to be said against this practice solely on the ground of brutality. Possibly any kind of fishing is brutal. But it need not be made unnecessarily so. And to break off tuna after tuna, making them drag hooks, leaders, lines around, marking them prey for sharks, would appear to an English angler as unsportsmanlike."

Billy Clover, a well-known boatman of San Pedro, arrived at Cape San Lucas Bay about a week after our arrival. He had been here several times, once as a guide and boatman for some California anglers. Clover's talk about his fishing experience in the Gulf was interesting, and his remarks on tackle most illuminating. The sum of the latter was that it was simply foolish to try to fish these waters with twenty-four-thread lines. Of course there were so many fish hooked that some, and quite large ones, would be caught, but nine out of ten broke away. Most of the three-hundred-pound tuna, and all the heavier ones, would be impossible to stop.

Clover claimed that April was not the best season for

Marlin. They worked up the coast and were most plentiful in summer. Broadbill swordfish frequented the Gulf, but never in great numbers. He harpooned one that was over twenty feet long and red in color. While he was towing it in the wind came up hard, making the sea so rough that the swordfish was torn away. This does not seem to me to be an exaggeration. Old *Xiphias Gladius* grows to enormous size and roams all the Seven Seas. Around the Marquesan Islands swordfish attain huge dimensions, according to some travelers. The natives there tell of swordfish with sword seven feet long. They attack and sink canoes, and kill fishermen. The Cubans also tell of a very large and dangerous swordfish. It is likely that these great swordfish inhabit only warm waters. How little is known of the Marlin, or spearfish, and the broadbill, the true swordfish! I have myself observed three different kinds of Marlin. No doubt there are others, all branches of the same family.

We raised seven Marlin in three days, without a strike. They were not hungry or did not like the kinds of bait we offered. Two of these were enormous black Marlin. I had my one strike up to this time on a needlefish.

While trolling to raise these fish we had our troubles with tuna. Every little while we would run over a school of tuna. Then, smash—crack! would go our teasers, no matter what kind. If we put out a baited hook we would soon have hold of a tuna. I caught several this way, one weighing one hundred and eighty-nine pounds. Romer caught two, one hundred and twenty-eight and one hundred and thirty-six, which feat amounted to a full day's work for him. Chester had a battle of two hours with a one hundred and ninety-five pounder. Captain Mitchell while trying to raise Marlin always had a bait out, and almost always he was hooking tuna.

It surely never lost its thrill for us—that flash of green and gold, the cracking splash, and then the tremendous lunge on the rod. And the run—what excitement and heat that roused!

One afternoon a vast school of blackfish, scattered all over the ocean, came down on us from the west. As far as we could see in every direction the big black snub noses and black hooked fins clove the blue water. At first we contented ourselves with chasing them to take pictures. But when it dawned on us that they in turn were chasing tuna, we remembered what wolves of the sea they were, and according to ichthyologists should be exterminated, and we got out the rifles.

Blackfish, or whale killers, were dangerous beasts. They really were not fish, but warm-blooded mammals, and in the experience of men who follow the sea, had been known to attack and sink boats.

I wasted a good deal of ammunition without doing them any harm. It was hard to shoot accurately from a bobbing boat. But at last I hit a huge ugly brute, and instantly wished I had missed him, for he heaved up, showing twenty feet of black bulk, and lunged in our direction. It did not matter whether this was accident or intent. Assuredly he was a fierce monster. He could have stove in our boat with his battering-ram of a head or smashed us with his wide flukes. I shot him twice in quick succession, hearing the impact of both bullets. Then he leaped. What a fearful creature! I yelled for Chester with all my might. But the other boat was some distance off, and Chester was busy with blackfish of his own. The one I had hit plunged back in a geyser of white water.

We ran over to where he had gone down. The water was colored. I saw the long, lean, gray-yellow shape of a leopard shark. Suddenly it appeared we were surrounded by blackfish, all from six to ten feet under the surface, but clearly distinguishable. Five of them swam under the boat. They were curious, even threatening. They did not rise to the surface. It was a pretty ticklish moment. Without word from me the boatman started both engines, full speed, and we shot away from there.

Next day the ocean off Cape San Lucas appeared to be a fishless waste. The tuna were gone. The blackfish had chased them away, or driven them down, or devoured them. My idea was that the tuna went down. Anyway, we did not see a tuna or have a strike. The net boats and live-bait boats caught no fish.

What unremittent strife goes on under the surface of the ocean! The big fish feed off the little ones. In these southern waters we found almost no fish feeding on the surface. In northern waters this is the rule, and it is a great help to the angler in locating fish.

One morning as we ran out off the Cape we espied a long dark line of leaping fish on the horizon. It was an inspiring sight, and we headed full speed toward it.

The sun was not more than an hour high, not over-bright, and the sea was smooth, fresh, cool, with a glimmering sun-track to the eastward. The fish looked black against the sky, mere dots at first, but gradually growing larger as we sped on. The even, regular motion of the line inclined me to the opinion that the fish were porpoises. They might well enough have been blackfish or dolphin. I stood up on deck and watched closely. When we were within two miles I decided the marching white and black wall was an enormous school of porpoises—by far the greatest number I had ever seen together. The school had fully a mile front. They were traveling northwest, and if they did not change their course or increase their speed would run right into us.

R. C.'s boat, with Chester on top at the motion-picture camera, beat us nearly half a mile, and were right upon them while we were yet far off. But we could see.

There were thousands of porpoises, of all sizes, apparently, and half of them appeared to be in the air when the other half was down. Occasionally a huge black-and-silver porpoise would leap high above the others and fall back, making a high splash. They did not leap like dolphin. The latter have a spiral motion, and these porpoises made a forward dive on their regular leap, and when they went high the action was just a dive directed up instead of ahead. The rhythmic motion and the flash of black, gold, silver above the white spray made a singularly beautiful sight.

I saw when Chester began to wind his camera. Then a few seconds later there suddenly came a sounding roar of water, quite distinct and different from anything I had ever heard. It was the same sound as that made by a school of mullet or flying-fish or sauer-fish, when they break water in front of a fiercely pursuing tarpon or barracuda or Marlin, only magnified tremendously. It was a sound of a multitude of sharp strong fish cutting water. The thousands of porpoises seemed actuated by a single idea. As one fish they leaped, faster and farther. Glittering, flying, disappearing, rank and file, whole columns like soldiers coming out together in a graceful parabolic curve, they thrilled the spectator as much as a great herd of caribou in the snow, or a rumbling herd of African buffalo crashing through the high grass.

We gave chase, and for several miles I could not see that we gained perceptibly. Our boats at top speed made about fourteen miles an hour. Gradually the porpoises slowed down, and we began to gain. R. C.'s boat went around to the north of the school, while my boat cut across to head them. Soon they were settling down to their regular gait and their playful water gymnastics. I saw porpoises leap twenty feet into the air, and farther than that on a straightaway forward dive. Usually it was a big fellow well in the lead that did the high leaping. A child could have seen that it was a playful jump.

R. C.'s boat turned the school to the eastward, almost straight at me. The front line of rounded shiny bodies was so wide that I could not get it all in my camera finder. Suddenly they again, "put it in high," as Bob said afterwards, and then the sight was inspiring. What action, life, rhythm! How the black backs and silver sides flashed! The roar, while yet a quarter of a mile distant, was so loud that we had to shout to hear each other.

We split the school and went with the larger half, that swerved to the southeast. Soon we were close. What wonderful leaps! Try as I would I could not snap a picture of one of these prodigious leaps. Always I would be pointing the camera at the wrong angle or I was not quick enough. The same applied to some of the lofty tumbles. I missed the best ones. But what excitement and fun I got out of it!

In a few moments we were surrounded by splashing, puffing, leaping gray bodies. Tiny baby porpoises leaped alongside huge plump ones, presumably their mothers. The roar of splitting water filled my ears. Sometimes a row of twenty would leap right in front of me. I would be looking down upon their glistening backs. The slapping of flat tails mingled with the roar.

They drew away from us, and sheering east, headed into the track of the sun. To our right came the other half of the school, soon to join those we had followed. Then we were afforded a scene of extraordinary beauty and life. The sunlight now was strong, the sea like a sheet of burnished silver, and the porpoises became black as ebony. What vigor, what strange freedom, what glit-

Rhinodon typus, or Whale Shark, Rarest Fish in the Seven Seas. Attains Length of Eighty Feet

PLATE CXI

FIGHTING *Rhinodon typus*

PLATE CXII

tering incessant action! Above the white splashes showered millions of sparkling drops, bright as diamonds. Thus the maelstrom distanced us and swept on into the glare of the sun.

That day I tried a new bait. I had caught a golden grouper, a fish of remarkably rich deep gold. It held its color, the skin was tougher than any other kind of fish we had used for bait, and it shone in the blue water with startling vividness. I was sure that if a Marlin sighted it he would take it whether he was hungry or not. Wherefore I trolled that bait between teasers of different kinds all day long. When the tuna were there that bait would not have lasted five minutes.

R. C. yelled and pointed ahead. Far out at sea I espied a leaping swordfish. Both boats made at top speed for him. Three jumps, far apart, was his contribution to our hopes. R. C.'s boat, as usual, forged ahead. Then out of the tail of my eye I saw a big splash right close. I did not get a glimpse of the fish. But I had the boat slowed down and the teasers thrown out. Then I let out my golden bait. We had not run fifty yards before I sighted a massive spear-pointed fish, bronze of back, purple of fin. He was coming like a straight flash. His thick body, large as a barrel, his incredible length, made my heart stand still. I yelled to the boatmen that it was one of the big black Marlins. He disappeared. We turned the boat and went back. Presently I felt a strong electrifying tug. What a shock it gave me! He let go. A deep whirling eddy appeared back of my bait. I waited in stinging hope. He did not come back. Perhaps the hook had stuck him. I bewailed my luck, my miserable fisherman's luck, my four-multiplying, triple-expansion, T.N.T.-voltage, ivory-tipped luck.

We worked that water well, then followed R. C. out

to sea. When he turned we ran alongside, and began to troll at our usual distance apart, always within call.

We heard R. C. shout. He pointed. To his right, ahead, showed the black tail of a Marlin cutting the swells. Bob ran R. C.'s boat a little too close to the fish and he swerved in our direction. I saw R. C. point and wave for me to try for him. Heisler shouted from the bow that he saw another fish. Anyway, before I had time to think, a purple shape, bird-like and as swift, flashed back of my left teaser. Winding in line I yelled for Sid to pull in the teaser. When my golden bait flashed into the place of the teaser the Marlin pounced upon it. As he sheered away I saw the bait between his jaws. Then away sped my line. I let him run two hundred feet. Then, throwing on the drag, I struck him hard and often. The solid live weight, the feel of the slipping line, the wagging of the rod, preceded his leap. It was a tearing splash, out of which he did not show clearly. But on the next he leaped magnificently, a light-colored Marlin of about four hundred pounds. We all greeted him with wild shouts. I was gratified to see that Chester was close to the fish, winding his camera. The thrill of the angler was on me. I watched almost breathlessly, while I handled the reel, trying to keep the line from getting loose. Impossible! This fish was everywhere, in and out, up and down. His twelfth leap was beautiful, high, straight up, and as he wagged his head I felt the tug on my line. He threw the hook and fell back, churned the water and was gone.

The boatmen were hard losers, and bemoaned our execrable luck. But I did not take this as a loss. That Marlin was a gentleman; he had sent my blood tingling; he had blazoned his exquisite white and silver and lilac colors against the blue sea. I could not ask any more.

CHAPTER XXII

WE had come to regard a certain place as the best
Marlin water in the vicinity. Probably it was
no better than any other locality thereabouts, but
having sighted more Marlin there we naturally went
back. Captain Heston told us that the hundred-fathom
bank directly off the Cape was the best swordfish ground.
We had not had any luck there. In the morning early
we trolled for bait off the steep wide beach of golden
sand along the east shore of the bay. Mackerel were
plentiful at times, and rarely we got a golden grouper.
The difficulty was to keep one of the big hundred-pound
cobias off the hook. This species of jewfish or bass, was
a hard fighter, and it was more work than fun to catch
him.

When we had caught some bait we ran down the shore,
off the rocky point, where the green swells roared and
crashed, out several miles into the Gulf. A red desert
headland, bleak and barren, furnished a landmark. Usually we trailed teasers behind the boat and watched
closely for Marlin. While the tuna were striking it was
not worth while to try to troll a bait for swordfish.

We had trolled all morning without sight of any kind

of a fish. The market boats had worked to the eastward, close inshore. The sea was dark blue, calm, and hot under the noonday sun. I was trying to keep from falling into a doze when Sid roused me:

"They're yellin' for us. Somthin' doin'."

At the same time he opened both throttles. I got up to face forward, with zest and the old curious thrill. R. C.'s boat was perhaps a quarter of a mile from us. R. C. was standing in the stern and instead of a rod he held his camera. Next instant I espied a high sharp black fin not far behind his boat. He yelled and waved for us to come.

"It's a basking shark, like we saw the other day," shouted Sid.

I thought so, too, but when we got within a hundred feet and I had a close view of that enormous fish I changed my mind. Still, it had the shape of a shark tail.

"What do you know about this?" yelled R. C. "Some fish! He's bigger than the boat. Doesn't seem to mind us."

Sid ran my boat closer. I saw white spots on the huge fin. It was not a fin, but the lobe of an enormous tail. I saw a silvery green mass, long and wide, with projections. The sunlight shining through the water upon this fish produced that peculiar green color. We always saw that green made when a whale was moving along under the surface. Then in another moment the green changed to a dark beautiful blue, dotted and streaked all over by a brilliant silver. The dorsal fin was low and stubby, the pectorals huge, apparently fan-shaped, almost resembling the wings of a colossal bat. The fish had a wide flat head, like that of a catfish, and he was close to sixty feet long. I recognized him as one of the rarest creatures in the sea—the *Rhineodon typus*, or whale shark. I had always wondered if I would ever have the luck to see one.

Dr. Gudger of the New York Natural History Museum is the authority on this strange fish, and he had sent me his fascinating booklet, containing all that was scientifically known about it.

In 1829 a Dr. Smith of South Africa harpooned a large shark of unusual appearance, and assisted by a number of men finally captured it. The shark was of unknown species. Dr. Smith named it *Rhineodon typus*.

This first specimen was fifteen feet long and nine in circumference. The skin was sent to the Paris Museum.

In 1850 Dr. Buist described a gigantic shark native to Kurrachee in northwest India, forty to sixty feet in length. This no doubt was the *Rhineodon typus*. In 1865 Dr. Gill described an enormous spotted shark of the Gulf of California, called by the natives "Tiburone ballenas," or "Whale shark." A specimen about twenty feet long was sent to the Smithsonian Institution.

In 1902 an eighteen-foot *Rhineodon* floated ashore at Ormond, Florida. From that year writers made frequent mention of the *Rhineodon;* and it became evident that the great shark had a wide distribution. Around the Seychelles Islands, north of Madagascar, this species was common. In the Indian Ocean it is called chagrin.

In 1912, Captain Thompson, a local boatman of Miami, Florida, captured a *Rhineodon* thirty-eight feet long. This fish was exhibited as an unknown sea monster, and was finally identified by Dr. Gudger. In 1924, my boatman, Captain Newton Knowles, with whom I have fished for years around Long Key, Florida, harpooned and killed a *Rhineodon* somewhat smaller than Thompson's.

Knowles told me there were two sharks together, and that the one he harpooned was much the smaller. An interesting statement was that the bridge-tender on the viaduct below Knight's Key informed Knowles he saw a number of these huge sharks every June. They came across the shoals from Florida Bay, and were working out into the Gulf Stream. Knowles said the shallow water made the capture of his fish a comparatively easy matter.

I remembered all this in a flash, while at the same time I was keen to photograph that lazy weaving black tail. I was afraid the fish would take fright and sound, but it paid not the slightest attention to either boat. We moved along very slowly, with the fish between us and a little ahead.

"What the devil is it?" called Bob King, leaning over the gunwale.

"*Rhineodon typus*," I replied, with the satisfaction of being able to classify what none of us had ever seen.

"By golly!" ejaculated Bob. "He shore ought to have a crazy name like that. He's the darndest-lookin' fish I ever saw. Let's ketch him!"

This instinct of capture might never have roused in me but for Bob. He could not see any kind of a fish, little or big, without wanting to catch it. Nevertheless, even as that boyish desire burned up in me, I knew perfectly well we could not hold such an enormous brute, if we did get fast to it.

We had one enormous gaff, and thought to get that in the shark. So, tying it to a heavy rope, we ran almost up on top of the fish. That afforded clearer view. The size was tremendous. From its dorsal fin to its head the length exceeded that of our boat, and it was wider than our beam. Lazily, with ponderous, slow weave of tail, it moved along, six or eight feet under the surface. Its dark blue color changed to a velvety brown, and the silver spots turned white. There was an exquisite purple along the edge of the broad pectoral fins. Altogether its colossal size, its singular beauty, its indifference to the boats, its suggestion of incredible power, made it the most wonderful fish I had ever seen.

"Good night!" called R. C., facetiously, as Heisler prepared to throw the gaff over the fish. "We'll pick up your remains in a minute."

I was standing on deck, beside Heisler, who wielded the heavy gaff. Up to that instant I had not thought of danger. The fish was harmless. But I realized that one blow from its tail could smash and sink us. What a strange cold prickle of my skin. I was all tight, breathless, staring, and as Heisler threw the gaff I suddenly sat down and held on to the hatch. Still I could see. The gaff sank over the side of the shark. Heisler pulled with all his might. It slipped off. The fish did not appear to be aware of our ambitious and evil intent. Bob was yelling, I know not what. R. C. and Chester had the cameras on us, and I was sure they were gleefully expecting to see us go flying into the air, with the debris of the boat. Heisler threw the gaff again. It would not stick. Twice more he failed to get a hold.

"Leave me have that gaff," yelled Bob. "I got six hundred feet of rope."

We gave it over to him quite with alacrity. Then we ran alongside, just a little behind. R. C. took the wheel of his boat, while Chester stood up on deck, at the camera.

"Don't blame me if we lose this Bell and Howell machine," he called, in grim humor.

Bob got out on the bow with the gaff. He had put it on the pole, and evidently did not intend to throw it loose on the rope, as Heisler had done. Bob motioned for R. C. to run the boat to suit him, and they drew up close to that weaving black tail. Bob lunged to gaff that tail. He got hold, but not securely. I stood breathlessly, pointing my camera, expecting to see something most startling. The fish did not change speed or position. His tail stuck six feet above the water. Bob took more time, waiting till the tail was right under him. Then he gaffed it. I saw the iron go through.

Next instant the tail disappeared in a waterspout. Then followed a thunderous crash that stopped my heart. But it was a sound of churning water. The shark had not hit the boat. I had been frightened out of securing a remarkable picture. The turmoil at the bow subsided. Then I saw Bob paying out rope, and huge bulges and swirls ahead of the boat. R. C. put on full speed, and so did Sid. We chased the *Rhineodon typus*. It was not a long chase, yet I felt I had never experienced one in any way similar. I could hardly believe what I saw. And I was convinced it would be over quickly. But that fish came up before long and swam on the surface as before. The gaff hook stuck there in the high black tail. We ran alongside and hailed that crew with excitement equal to their own.

Bob got Chester to hold the rope, while he went below. I divined at once that he meant to rig up some kind of an iron. Bob had a reputation in Florida for catching huge rays, sharks, manatees, alligators; and I knew he was bent on outdoing the feats of Thompson and Knowles. Chester had been left a Herculean task. But he was valiant. And when he lost rope R. C. would run the boat ahead so that he recovered it. Sometimes the black tail would slap against the bow.

Presently Bob appeared with some kind of a spear rigged from a file that had been bound on a gaff pole. He attached a rope to the spear. Then with business-like promptness he plunged the thing into the fish. He shoved down on it with all his might. The shark made a roaring hole in the sea, almost large enough to swamp the boat. Then he sounded. R. C.'s boat ran to the edge of the maelstrom and stopped. Quickly the water smoothed out, hissing and seething. Both ropes went slipping over the gunwale until several hundred feet were gone. Gradually then the shark slowed until he stopped. With that Bob signaled us to come alongside.

"Go back to the ship an' fetch ropes, barrels, harpoons, guns," he called. "We'll ketch this rhinoceros tappus."

I tried to persuade Bob that we had no equipment equal to the job.

"Shore we can ketch him," he replied, with a keen flash of his blue eyes.

"But the water is deep," I protested. "Those few that have been caught were found in shallow water."

"This bird will come up," averred Bob. "We'll get a couple more holds, then when he comes to the surface break his back with bullets. Bring your heavy guns."

"But there's danger—leaving you here alone," I replied, hesitating.

"Give you my word we'll keep away from him," said Bob.

At that assurance I consented and we headed towards the bay at a speed never before equaled by the little boat. The stern sunk down level with the water and the bow stood high. How the engines roared! It was impossible for me not to revel in the whole proceeding, however preposterous it was.

Upon reaching the ship we created a great deal of excitement by our hurry, and what seemed mysterious conduct.

"Get Romer, Johnny, Captain Mitchell," I yelled, and rushed to my cabin for guns and shells, more films, a heavy coat, and a flash light. Heisler was to get the other things Bob wanted. When I emerged Romer and Johnny met me wild with excitement and curiosity.

"We're hooked on to a *Rhineodon typus* sixty feet long," I said, in answer to their queries.

"What on earth's that?" shouted Romer. "Where? How? When? Is it a sea serpent?"

"Get your coats. Hustle," was all the satisfaction I gave them.

In a few moments we were again aboard the little boat. Captain Mitchell forgot his hat. Everybody left on board cheered from the rail. We shot off to the eastward between two sheets of spray. Then I had time to tell the boys what a *Rhineodon typus* was and how we had come to get tangled up with one. If anything this information only served to make them wilder.

We expected any moment to see R. C.'s boat coming back. But we were mistaken, and when finally I sighted it, a dot on the horizon, it appeared to be stationary. They were still fast to the fish. We were thirty-five minutes getting back to R. C.'s boat. They waved and yelled a welcome. I believed R. C. looked relieved. The shark was on the surface, tail and dorsal out, and it was towing the boat.

We gaily hailed R. C. and his men, and running close put Captain Mitchell aboard his boat. Before I could ask Bob what the next procedure should be R. C. pointed out to sea and said:

"I hate to make you feel bad," he said. "But look there."

I looked hastily, with eager thrill. But before I saw anything except water Romer let out a wild yell. "Look! Look! Big Marlin! Oh, he's a whale. Right there!"

Presently I espied the short stubby black fin and the long blade-like tail of a Marlin. The striking thing was the extreme length between dorsal and tail. Fully ten feet! Then the low dorsal and dark color proclaimed the fish a black Marlin. He lay on the surface some two hundred yards out, evidently sunning himself on the glassy sea.

"Boys, you'll have to dispense with our services for a little while," I said. "Here, Bob, take all this truck we brought."

"Gimme some rope an' a keg," replied Bob. "You go an' ketch that Marlin. We'll wait. Our Rhinoceros is millin' round nowhere in particular."

My rod and baited hook lay in the cockpit, just where I had placed them when we quit trolling. Taking them up, I instructed Sid to run round that Marlin so I could drag my golden bait in front of him. When we were about two hundred feet from him I happened to remember the teasers.

"Throw the teasers out," I shouted. "Slow down a little. There. Now keep away from him."

Scarcely had the port teaser begun to twinkle and flash in the wake of the launch when the Marlin woke up and disappeared in a heavy swirl. But I had seen him head toward us.

"Boys, he's coming. He saw the teaser," I said, excitedly, as I frantically wound my bait in. I had let out perhaps sixty feet of line. In that few seconds, before I could reel my bait close to the teaser, the dark purple flash of that Marlin appeared between my bait and the teaser. With what bullet-speed he had come! His thick black dorsal showed above the surface. To and fro he weaved, with the marvelous quickness peculiar to this fish. A few more turns of my reel brought the golden bait in front of the Marlin. He snapped it in, sheered away, leaving a violent swirl in the water. The moment was singularly thrilling. I thought I was cool, but most likely made a mistake. My legs shook as I sat down to drop the rodbutt in the seat-socket. The line whizzed off the reel. When I was about to strike the line went slack. He had spit out the bait. I had let him have it too long. Romer's disappointment exceeded mine, which was great enough. "You let him run too far!" And Sid's comment was similar in import. "These Marlin don't take a cut bait like they do a flying-fish. You ought to have hit him quick."

"A bird in hand is worth two in the bush," observed Johnny, sagely.

Forthwith I forgot another wonderful opportunity to catch a great Marlin; and we sped back to R. C.'s boat.

"He sure was hungry. It was some strike. Too bad!" said R. C.

"These Marlin are like sailfish," added Bob. "You want to soak them when they turn away with the hook. How big was he?"

"I couldn't be sure, but over five hundred, anyway. . . . What shall we do now?"

"Jab a couple of irons into this Rhinoceros," replied Bob, and he instructed Heisler just where and how to hit the shark.

We ran ahead, alongside our quarry, now with dorsal out of the water. I discarded camera for rifle. With calmer eye I judged the *Rhineodon* to exceed fifty feet in length, at the most conservative estimate. But if he had shrunk a little in size he still retained his strange beauty. We drew close, with the bow at his head. Heisler lunged down with the pole. It was as if he had struck a rock. The iron came back bent. While Heisler hammered it straight the huge fish swam on unconcernedly. Soon Heisler was ready for another try. We had grown somewhat hardened to the presence of the *Rhineodon* and therefore less fearful. We ran right alongside it, so that I had the most wonderful sight of this marine monster. Heisler repeated his harpooning performance, with all the violence of which he was capable. Crash went the mighty tail. We were deluged with water. Everybody on both boats appeared to be yelling hoarse instructions.

I heard the impact of the fish against the boat. "Hold on!" yelled Heisler. I thought he meant for the boys to stay with him at the rope. But when the boat began to rise out of the water I knew differently. Then with the lifting motion came a tremendous scraping on the bottom of the boat. The shark had swerved under us. The boys fell with Heisler, all hanging to the rope. I came within an inch of going overboard, but managed desperately to cling to a ring-bolt until the launch righted. Then the threshing, thumping tail appeared above water on our port side. What a narrow escape! The iron pulled out, the rope slackened; and that enabled us to run from in front of Bob, who was swearing lustily. When we got in good position again Bob called for Heisler to come aboard his launch. Still the *Rhineodon* stayed on the surface. Bob was soon ready, and we followed close beside his boat. The shark was moving faster now, though still high in the water. While Heisler, Chester, and Mitchell held the ropes, Bob plunged the iron deep back of the dorsal. Roar of beaten water, flooded bobbing boats, blinded fishermen! Pandemonium prevailed for a few seconds, until the deluge subsided. That was surely the most terrific moment in all my fishing experience. My blood ran cold, my heart seemed to freeze, then burst. I had most thought of Romer. But he, with strong brown hands hung on to that boat with the grim zest of passionate, fearless youth. Above the other noise I heard his piercing yell to Johnny, who was likewise strenuously engaged. I had one knee locked on the engine hatch, and my other leg hung overboard. The rifle had fallen, luckily to catch along the rail. When I extricated myself I was relieved to see that the *Rhineodon* had sounded, and was taking line with remarkable swiftness compared to his former movements. Bob had two ropes

[213]

and Heisler had one.   Chester and Mitchell were very
busy getting out other ropes.

At about six hundred feet the shark stopped, and
swam on at that depth, towing the boat for miles an
hour.   Presently, at Bob's word, the four men began to
haul in on the ropes.   It was a slow, laborsome task.
The ropes had to be coiled in tubs as they came in.   The
afternoon was still and hot.   Red-faced, and dripping
sweat, the men worked incessantly.   It took an hour to
pull the *Rhineodon* to the surface.   How funny to see
the big gaff-hook waving in that black tail!   He towed
the boat a couple of miles inshore, and then to the westward.   Then he sounded.   The men had a harder job to
haul him up.   They were wringing wet, and Bob, who
had labored longest, was a sight to behold.

To make a long story short, they fought that fish until
nearly sunset, during which it sounded five times, going
deeper every time, the last being over twelve hundred
feet.

When they got him up again Bob yelled to me, "Come
aboard this boat with your big rifle."   We ran up to
them and I went aboard, together with Romer and
Johnny.   While I watched for a chance to shoot, the
boys pitched in to help.   But the *Rhineodon* did not
come to the surface enough for me to disable it, even
with the big fifty caliber.

Sunset came.   Our quarry manifestly thought it was
his bedtime, for he suddenly sounded.   The ropes sped
down.   Different lengths of rope, tied together, marked
how many feet he descended.   Six hundred!   Twelve
hundred!   Fifteen!   Two of the tubs went overboard
to sink.   Heisler made a Herculean effort to save his
tub, but it could not be done.   As the end of the rope
left his hands he kicked the tub overboard.   Some one

else had the white line to which the tub-rope was attached.

Down, slower and slower, but surely inevitably down, the great shark sounded. The boys, with Chester and Mitchell, strove frantically to save a new rope from following the others. In vain! Foot by foot it slipped through their wet, grimy gloved hands. Bob had his rope under the cleat on the bow. He too was in desperate straits, but not vanquished.

Here I put aside my rifle and entered the fray. The spirit to conquer that brute was contagious. When the last few feet of new rope lay in sight, Chester hurriedly tied the last ball of white line to the end. Bob was panting and swearing. "More rope! . . . We'll lick him yet. Somebody get more rope. I'm losin' heah."

"Just tied on the last piece," replied Chester.

Then followed a short intense struggle to stop the fish, before he had all the rope. Heisler nearly went overboard hanging on to his, but he lost it. That was the last I saw clearly, for my eyes grew red with the effort I was making. We knew indeed we were whipped, at least all of us knew except Bob. For when I gave the order to take a half hitch with the ropes and let the fish pull free of the irons Bob groaned loudly. Then he panted: "Got to—hand it—to old Rhinoceros. I've more—respect for him—than I started with."

Upon comparing notes we found that we had seen four *Rhineodon typus* close to the vicinity where the battle had taken place.

Takahashi visited the Japanese fishermen and returned with some interesting information. Two of the large net boats had been towed by one of these sharks for eighteen hours before it broke away. Another net boat caught a fifty-four-foot *Rhineodon* in their net, and turned it loose.

The market fishermen saw a number of them every season in the Gulf of California, and they were especially numerous on the east shore of Santa Margarita Island.

This news only added to the sum of wonderful fish in those southern waters, and fanned the flame of my desire to visit them again, with better equipment and more time, so that all the marvelous fishing possibilities could be realized.

THE END